THE MEAT STRETCHER MEAL GUIDE...

FOR BUDGET MINDED, HEALTH CONSCIOUS COOKS

SPECIAL Calorie and Cholesterol Charts

Over 175 Recipes

TOMI RYAN &
JAMES H. RYAN, M.D.

FIRST EDITION

First Printing: May 1975

OTHER BOOKS BY THE AUTHORS:

The Meatless Meal Guide
  for budget-minded, health conscious cooks
The Great Cook Writes a Book
Gourmet My Way

PUBLISHED BY:

THE RYAN COMPANY

2188 Latimer Lane, Los Angeles, Ca. 90024

Copyright © 1975 by James H. Ryan, M.D.

ISBN: 0-914202-03-0

This Book

Is

Dedicated

To

Our Parents

Who have enriched our lives

In so many ways

Colored Text Paper:
  Wausau Paper Comapny's 70# Exact Matte

Printed in the USA by:
  ColorGraphics Inc., Los Angeles

Bound in the USA by:
  Dependable Folding & Binding Co., Los Angeles

Graphic Artist:
  Mr. Tim Bryant

CONTENTS

INTRODUCTION

"The choice is only, whether one will eat good or ill"

J.C. Loudon, 1826

The typical American diet, as well as the diets of most developed countries, may be doing more harm than good. There is nothing new or particularly startling in this statement. The fact is, too many are consuming too much of the wrong foods. Foods too high in calories, saturated fat, cholesterol and refined sugar; along with foods lacking in essential nutrients and natural fiber content. This is happening inspite of the abundance and availability of highly nutritious foods. Our dietary problems stem from both ignorance and a contentment with making the wrong food choices.

The health of the entire family, to a large degree, is determined by the food choices made at the supermarket and what is happening in the kitchen. A prolonged faulty diet flirts with illness and possible disaster. Obesity and hypertension are shortening lives and premature heart attacks are striking men down during their prime years. These three illnesses are the overriding public health concerns in America today. The foods we eat play important roles in all of them. MEAT STRETCHER MEALS must be considered in light of the current findings of medical and nutritional research.

The outlook for a healthier nation has never been better. The high cost of food, especially meat, has riveted our focus on getting the most nutrition out of each food dollar spent. Budget-minded, health-conscious cooks are now overhauling their meat-rich meals to meet this challenge. De-emphasizing meat helps remove excess calories, saturated fat and cholesterol from our diets. This can easily be done without jeoprodizing protein intake. A cup of non-fat milk and a peanut butter sandwich may provide over 1/3 of the adult male's daily protein requirement and close to ½ of the adult female's. In addition, MEAT STRETCHER MEALS and MEATLESS MEALS play important roles in the global struggle against hunger, malnutrition and starvation. You will discover the good life on a budget and eat healthier and better meals when consuming less meat.

Modernizing our diets through nutritional education is the key to healthier and longer lives. Teaching good nutrition to children is critical, since coronary heart disease and obesity problems may often be traced to poor eating habits established during childhood. Eating healthy foods was the pattern Tomi and I established for each of our fifteen foster babies and is the reason for Tomi's present involvement with children's cooking classes - classes designed to "Make Big Chefs out of Little People" in delicious and nutritious ways.

The **MEAT STRETCHER** recipes, the nutritional information, and the calorie and cholesterol charts found in this book, together with the recipes and information from our book **THE MEATLESS MEAL GUIDE**, should be helpful in reducing an abnormally high blood cholesterol and in lowering and maintaining a normal weight. This has been my personal experience. With practice, persistence and careful planning you too may achieve the same satisfying results. How well your body functions and how long it will last is up to you. I can only assure you, as did the 16th-century English physician Thomas Moffet assure his readers: " 'Tis not an Itch to be in Print but my Profession to keep Men alive that hath induced me to the Undertaking."

Los Angeles, California

James H. Ryan, M.D.

"Healthy Meals are Happy Meals"

ATTACKING THE HEART ATTACK

"O, Worshipful one! Which of the three types of ailments of the patient does the physician treat - the past ailment, the present one or the future one?"

CARAKA SAMHITA, an ancient Hindu medical book

The heart attack rate has risen so explosively in this century that coronary heart disease is now epidemic and mankind's most deadly disease. The underlying disease process, known as atherosclerosis, develops slowly and silently, then, generally without warning, strikes with a vengeance. The awesome toll is 700,000 American lives annually - accounting for 1 out of every 2 deaths in this country. Of those struck, 20% die in the first hour and over 30% die before ever reaching a hospital. The hope for the future lies not only in faster and better treatment, but in starting preventive measures before one becomes a casualty.

Of the four major coronary risk factors - high blood cholesterol, high blood pressure, heavy cigarette smoking and overweight - an elevated cholesterol is probably the risk factor easiest to change and control. The heavy consumption of saturated fats and cholesterol, obtained principally from meat and meat products, is one of the main reasons our cholesterol levels are too high. High blood cholesterols are also associated with overweight. Fortunately, the diet changes needed to reduce one's cholesterol also work to hold calories and weight in check. Planning and eating a diet low in cholesterol and saturated fat is neither painful nor costly. On the contrary, MEAT STRETCHER MEALS and MEATLESS MEALS are easy to prepare, nutritious, delicious, low in calories and inexpensive.

Don't put off what you can do now to protect your family's hearts for the future. There are no guarantees that a change in the diet will prevent heart attack, but it could increase your survival chances. No one is invulnerable.

Try Prevention

FACTS ON FATS

> "The doctor of the future will give no medicines, but will interest his patients in the care of the human frame, in diet, and in the cause and prevention of disease."
>
> Thomas A. Edison

Fats are important dietary constituents because of their high energy value, supply of fat-soluble vitamins, essential fatty acids and palatability. However, excessive fat consumption is predisposing to obesity, high blood cholesterol and heart attack. With the fat content of the American diet having nearly doubled in the last 75 years, medical experts, the American Heart Association and the American Medical Association are now urging everyone to lower their fat calorie intake from the present 45 to 50% of the day's total calories to around 30%. Significantly, the Japanese have 6 times fewer heart attacks than Americans and their diets contain less than 5% meat and about 10% fat. The Calorie Counter beginning on page 193 permits gram for gram comparisons of the fat, carbohydrate and protein values found in our foods. To convert grams of fat to calories of fat, multiply the number of fat grams by 9.

There are two types of fats in the diet we must be aware of. First, the saturated fats or "solid" fats of animal origin found in meats, eggs, whole milk, butter, cream and hard cheeses. Second, the polyunsaturated fats or liquid oils of vegetable origin obtained from seeds, nuts and vegetable oil products. Saturated fats push up blood cholesterol levels. Polyunsaturated fats pull down cholesterol levels. Polyunsaturated fats may be "hardened" into saturated fats by a chemical process called hydrogenation. Hydrogenated vegetable oil products are counted as saturated fats. Partial hydrogenation retains varying amounts of polyunsaturated fats, anywhere from 25% to over 60%, as in soft margarines. Product labels list the major ingredients first, thereby indicating whether saturated, hydrogenated, partially hydrogenated, or polyunsaturated fats (liquid vegetable oils) predominate. Margarines are comparable to butter in calories unless otherwise noted on the package, as may be the case with special or diet margarines. A diet containing fats in the ratio of 1/3 saturated fats to 2/3 polyunsaturated fats is considered desirable.

Cut
Fats

CHOLESTEROL COUNTS

"A man is as old as his arteries."
Thomas Sydenham, M.D., 17th century

The main coronary arteries, 5 inches long and ¼ inch in diameter, are the lifelines which supply the heart muscle with blood. The inner walls of these arteries are subject to the build-up of cholesterol-laden deposits, or plaques, which lay the foundation for heart attack. As the plaques slowly thicken, roughen and harden, the blood flow through one of the coronary arteries may become insufficient for the heart under stress, or the flow may become shut-off completely, or blocked by a blood clot, or interrupted by the rupture of the artery wall. The result is a "coronary," "coronary thrombosis," "acute myocardial infarction," or more commonly "heart attack." The disease process, called atherosclerosis, is universally known as "hardening of the arteries."

Cholesterol is an important fatty substance normally found in the blood and manufactured by the liver. The blood cholesterol level is also affected by the foods we eat, particularly meats, eggs, butter, gravies, shellfish, pastries and desserts. The average blood cholesterol level in the United States was 180 milligrams, but now stands near 250 milligrams. Medical studies have repeatedly shown that the higher the cholesterol level the greater the risk of heart attack. A change from our present dietary intake of around 700 to 800 milligrams of cholesterol per day to less than one-half this amount has been recommended by health experts as an important step in reducing and maintaining lower blood cholesterol levels. Those persons engaged in vigorous physical labor or exercise usually have no cholesterol problem and are possible exceptions.

The cholesterol content in our foods varies widely: a four ounce serving of meat contains over 100 milligrams, 3 ounces of liver 370, 3 ounces of Halibut 50, one egg yolk 250, one cream puff with custard 190, 1 tablespoon butter 35, margarine 0, all fruits 0, all vegetables 0. A healthy solution is to eat more fruits and vegetables, fish and poultry, nuts and peanut butter, breads and cereals, skim milk and uncreamed cottage cheese, and substitute more margarine for butter and vegetable oils for lard. For help in planning low-cholesterol meals use the Cholesterol Counter beginning on page 201. Since meat and meat products are a major source of both saturated fats and cholesterol, we suggest you s-t-r-e-t-c-h it!

Kick the
Cholesterol
Habit

"Greater Numbers dig their Graves with their own Teeth and die more
by those fatal Instruments, than the Weapons of their Enemies."
MOFFET ON FOOD, published 1655

The overconsumption of calories has become one of man's great enemies. The overweight person is more prone to heart disease, high blood pressure, diabetes and other life shortening conditions; and is a greater surgical risk. Crash-fad dieting is not the answer, it is doomed to failure, and may be harmful to your health. The estimate is that less than 1% of fad dieters loose weight permanently. Consult your physician when in search of sensible dieting.

Calorie control is the indispensible ingredient in any weight control program. This does not mean other important nutritional factors can be ignored, or minimized, when reducing and maintaining one's weight. If good health is to be maintained, one must count calories, control portions and know something about the nutritional composition of foods. Since foods overlap in nutrition values, meeting daily nutritional needs can be simplified by using the BASIC FOUR PLUS ONE FOOD GROUPS on page 13 as a meal planning guide. When one cuts back on calorie consumption, the PLUS FOODS need careful management if nutritional deficiencies are to be prevented. Calorie control can be pleasureable and palatable, and more likely to last a lifetime, if you select the foods you like in a wise and precise manner. Our recipes should help you discover this important fact.

Building new eating habits and increasing one's physical activity are two other essential diet ingredients. Stop, what I call "The Gulping Syndrome." It is amazing how much less food you crave, and how enjoyable food becomes, when you eat slowly. Also, discover how easy it is to be satisfied with thinner slices and smaller portions of meat and other high calorie foods, especially when eaten slowly and served on smaller plates. Always ask yourself, "Do I need this big of a piece?" Although an overall increase in physical activity makes a meaningful contribution to reducing and controlling weight, remember it is far easier to eliminate calories than to exercise them off. How many calories can be burned-up per hour doing physical exercise? About 75 to 100 by sedentary activities such as light house

Obesity
Is
Preventable

and office work; 150 to 250 by moderate activities such as bed making, light gardening, and moderately fast walking; 250 to 350 by more vigorous work and activities such as heavy household chores, walking fast, gardening, golfing and bowling; over 350 by strenuous activities such as running, bicycling, energetic dancing, football, tennis, ice skating and swimming.

The key to permanent weight loss is to embrace calorie watching as a way of life. One pound of extra fat contains 3500 calories. You must consume 3500 less calories, or burn-up 3500 more calories, to lose a pound of excess weight. To lose one pound per week take in 500 less calories per day than your body requires, and 1000 less calories per day to lose two pounds a week. Since no foolproof calorie counting method exists, try a Calorie Countdown System. Instead of adding calories up, subtract the calories you eat from your days allowance as you eat. Then you know exactly how many more calories to look forward to the rest of the day. Attention is thus focused on planning and stretching the remaining calories for maximum nutrition and enjoyment. Leftover calories may be "banked" as bonus, or reserve, calories for the weekend or some special occasion.

It should be noted by those only 8 to 10 pounds overweight: a daily decrease of just 100 calories, or about one ounce less meat per day, results in 35,000 fewer calories a year. This is equivalent to a 10 pound weight loss for the year. Trimming off these extra pounds will not only make you feel better but help stretch the family's food budget.

Nutrition affects all phases of our lives. During the early years, when our bodies are rapidly growing and developing, we acquire the fat cells and eating habits that may come to haunt us the rest of our lives. One of the most important things you can do for a child is to introduce them to a wide variety of healthy foods, preferably in the preschool years, and then teach them which foods and amounts are best for them. You can demonstrate your concern for good nutrition and responsibility by setting a good example.

Gram for gram, fats contain twice as many calories as proteins and carbohydrates. Therefore, one should be stingy with meats and fats and generous with fruits and vegetables. It is helpful to keep a list of your favorite low-calorie foods and recipes handy. When in doubt about calorie counts and portion sizes consult the Calorie Counter on page 193. The Calorie Counter also contains useful information on the protein, carbohydrate and fat content of many common foods. Determine your ideal weight from the chart on page 11.

Choose
Healthy
Calories

DESIRABLE WEIGHT CHARTS

DESIRABLE WEIGHTS FOR MEN AND WOMEN AGED 25 AND OVER
in pounds according to height and frame (in indoor clothing)

HEIGHT		SMALL FRAME	MEDIUM FRAME	LARGE FRAME
MEN				
Feet	Inches			
5	2	112-120	118-129	126-141
5	3	115-123	121-133	129-144
5	4	118-126	124-136	132-148
5	5	121-129	127-139	135-152
5	6	124-133	130-143	138-156
5	7	128-137	134-147	142-161
5	8	132-141	138-152	147-166
5	9	136-145	142-156	151-170
5	10	140-150	146-160	155-174
5	11	144-154	150-165	159-179
6	0	148-158	154-170	164-184
6	1	152-162	158-175	168-189
6	2	156-167	162-180	173-194
6	3	160-171	167-185	178-199
6	4	164-175	172-190	182-204

HEIGHT		SMALL FRAME	MEDIUM FRAME	LARGE FRAME
WOMEN				
Feet	Inches			
4	10	92- 98	96-107	104-119
4	11	94-101	98-110	106-122
5	0	96-104	101-113	109-125
5	1	99-107	104-116	112-128
5	2	102-110	107-119	115-131
5	3	105-113	110-122	118 134
5	4	108-116	113-126	121-138
5	5	111-119	116-130	125-142
5	6	114-123	120-135	129-146
5	7	118-127	124-139	133-150
5	8	122-131	128-143	137-154
5	9	126-135	132-147	141-158
5	10	130-140	136-151	145-163
5	11	134-144	140-155	149-168
6	0	138-148	144-159	153-173

PUTTING IT ALL TOGETHER

"Doctors are always working to preserve health and cooks to destroy
it ... the latter are more often successful."
>   Denis Diderot, 18th century French philosopher

Budget-minded, health-conscious cooks are now on the move against diets injurious to health. And in the wake, they are discovering nutritious meals need not be expensive meals. Concerned cooks are also realizing preventive eating may hold the most important key to a longer, healthier and happier life, especially when begun in childhood. It is not only wise to take precautions against nutritional deficiencies, obesity and heart attack, but may even be urgent for the flabby, overweight, overstressed, heavy smoking, hypertensive and inactive male in his 40's. A PREVENT DIET plan for good health should include the whole family and take into consideration the following:

1. **TO PREVENT** nutritional deficiencies and to meet or exceed the daily minimum nutritional requirements, eat from a well-choosen, wide variety of foods. Use our **BASIC FOUR PLUS ONE FOOD GROUPS** (next page) as a meal planning guide.

2. **TO CHECK** excess weight keep your calorie intake, calorie requirements and physical exercise in balance. Let the information on pages 9 & 10 and the Calorie Counter on page 193 help you master calorie counting and weight watching.

3. **TO MINIMIZE** the cholesterol risk factor in heart disease, eat lean meat, stretch the meat you eat, and use the information on page 8 and the Cholesterol Counter on page 201 to help you plan low-cholesterol meals. Contact your physician or local Chapter of the American Heart Association for more information.

4. **TO MAINTAIN** fat intake at the desired level of 1/3 of the day's calories use the information on page 7 and the Calorie Counter on page 193.

5. **TO AVOID** other dietary pitfalls cut back on refined sugar, sugar-rich "junk" foods and markedly increase the amount of fiberous foods in the diet.

6. **TO MAXIMIZE** your family's health learn all you can about good nutrition from authoritative sources.

Eat
Preventively

Bran muffins

use few baking makes
dough loose ..   400°   15 min
1 C milk
1 egg   * add raisins last
1 T Honey   nuts
2T malases
1 C co wh flour
1 C millers Bran
4 T Baking Powder

(Put rising agent in last
as it starts the action
too soon)

(Soak overnight lwte
plump raisins in orange juice
or Bail in water 5 min)
          orange

mix liquid mixture in
bowl

add all dry ingredients
then last put in Baking
Powder. Mix into dry
mixture (on top) well --
then mix into all
liquid

BASIC FOUR FOOD GROUPS

PLUS FOOD GROUP

VEGETABLE & FRUIT GROUP

Plan at least 4 half cup servings to include both raw and cooked. Include a citrus fruit, tomato or other good source of vitamin C everyday, and every other day a dark-green or deep-yellow vegetable for vitamin A.

Count as one serving: 1 medium apple, banana, orange or potato, half a medium grapefruit or cantaloup.

4 or more
half cup servings daily

MILK GROUP

Children	3-4 glasses (8 oz.)
Teenager	4 or more glasses
Adult	2 or more glasses

Alternatives: 1-inch cube cheddar-type cheese, ¾ cup cottage cheese, ice milk, ice cream, or yogurt may replace ½ glass of fluid milk (4 oz.).

Preference should be given to low-fat dairy products.

2-4 or more
8-ounce glasses daily

This group contributes insignificant amounts of nutrients, but adds substantial amounts of calories, costs & saturated fats when eaten to excess.

Sugar - Sweets (sugar = 40 calories per T.)
  Sugar, honey & molasses
  Jams, jellies & marmalades
  Party & fun foods
   cookies & candies
  Desserts & snacks
  Soft drinks
  Alcholic beverages

Fats - Oils (fats = 125 calories per T.)
  Bacon
  Commercial baked foods
   doughnuts & sweet rolls
   biscuits & muffins
  Butter & maragrine
  Lard & vegetable shortenings
  Oils & salad dressings
  Mayonnaise & tartar sauce

BREAD & CEREAL GROUP

Whole grain or enriched breads and cereals, other homemade baked foods made with enriched or whole grain flour, enriched rice, macaroni, spaghetti and noodles.

A serving is 1 slice of enriched or whole grain bread, ½ to ¾ cup whole grain or fortified cereal, or ½ cup cooked rice or cooked macaroni product.

4 or more
servings daily

MEAT GROUP

Lean cooked meat, poultry, fish, shellfish and eggs.
1 egg is equal in amount of protein to 1-ounce lean cooked meat. Limit eggs to 3-5 per week.

Alternatives: ½ cup dried beans, peas, lentils, 2 T. peanut butter may replace ½ serving of meat. All types of nuts may also be substituted.

2 servings daily
to total 5 to 6-ounces

Many of these items are used as recipe ingredients or additions to other foods. Regulate this group for calorie control.

As needed to supply enough calories (food energy) and to make meals more palatable

BEEF CUTS

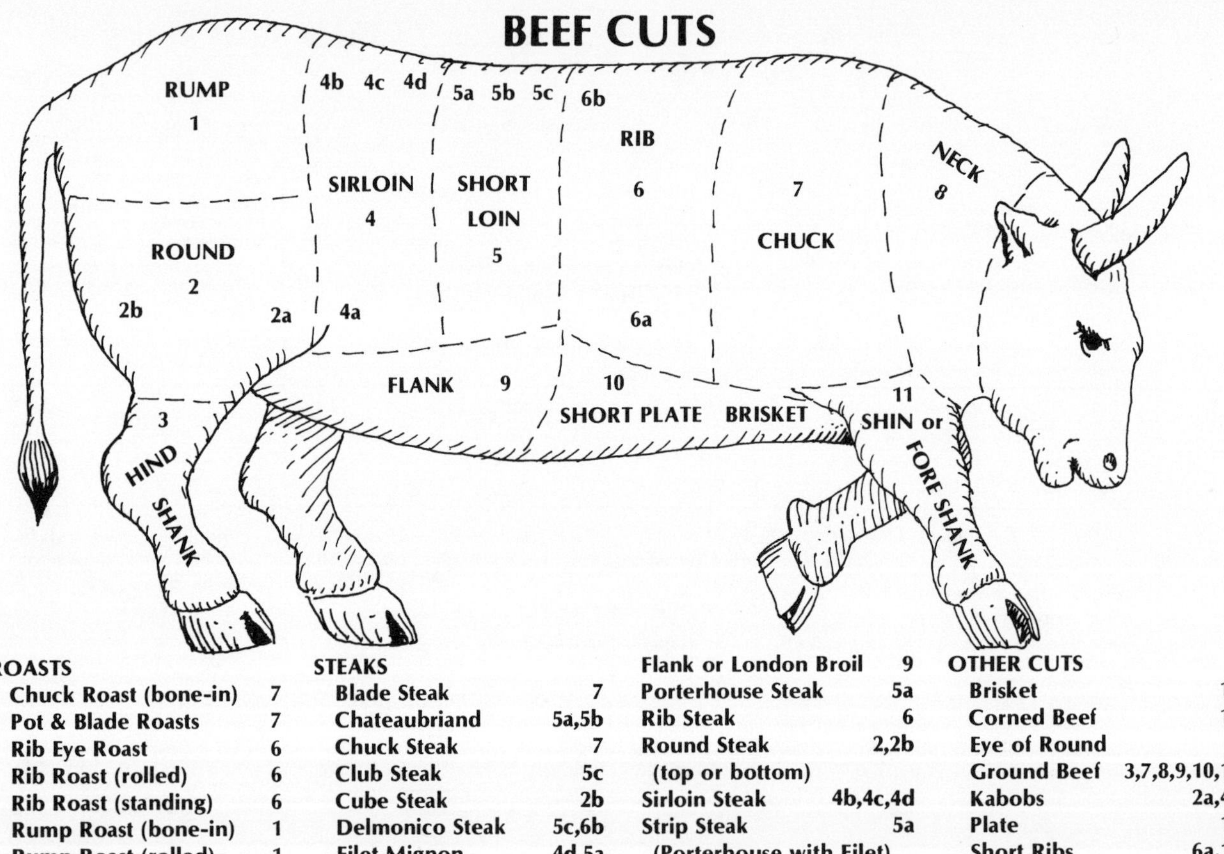

ROASTS		STEAKS		Flank or London Broil	9	OTHER CUTS	
Chuck Roast (bone-in)	7	Blade Steak	7	Porterhouse Steak	5a	Brisket	10
Pot & Blade Roasts	7	Chateaubriand	5a,5b	Rib Steak	6	Corned Beef	10
Rib Eye Roast	6	Chuck Steak	7	Round Steak	2,2b	Eye of Round	2
Rib Roast (rolled)	6	Club Steak	5c	(top or bottom)		Ground Beef	3,7,8,9,10,11
Rib Roast (standing)	6	Cube Steak	2b	Sirloin Steak	4b,4c,4d	Kabobs	2a,4a
Rump Roast (bone-in)	1	Delmonico Steak	5c,6b	Strip Steak	5a	Plate	10
Rump Roast (rolled)	1	Filet Mignon	4d,5a	(Porterhouse with Filet)		Short Ribs	6a,10
Sirloin Tip Roast	2a,4a	(Tenderloin)		T-Bone Steak	5b	Stew Meat	3,7,8,9,10,11

THE RECIPES

" 'Tis not the meat, but 'tis the appetite
Makes eating a delight."

Sir John Suckling, 1642
FRAGMENTA AUREA

"How beautiful the universe when something digestible meets
with an eager digestion."

Don Marquis (1878-1937)

"The pleasures of the table are for every man, of every land,
and no matter of what place in history or society."

Anthelme Brillat-Savarin (1755-1826)
French gastronomist

We encourage you to alter the recipes to satisfy your own taste and health
preferences and to substitute with ingredients on hand.

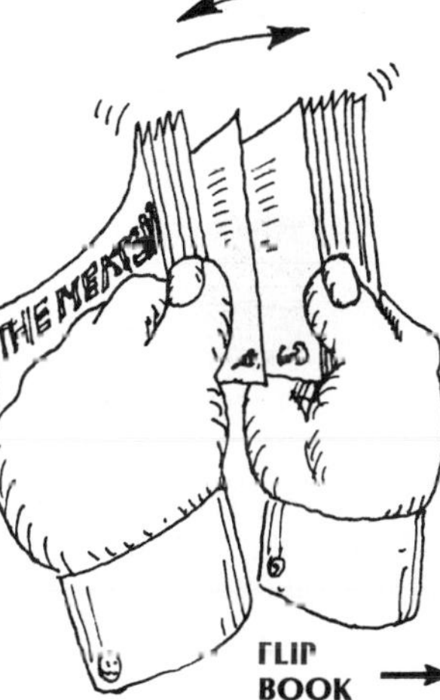

ABBREVIATIONS

c.	= cup	oz.	= ounce
cond.	= condensed	opt.	= optional
env.	= envelope	pd.	= powder
fr.	= frozen	pkg.	= package
grad.	= gradually	qt.	= quart
hr.	= hour	refrig.	= refrigerate
ingred.	= ingredients	sm.	= small
lb.	= pound	t.	= teaspoon
lg.	= large	T.	= tablespoon
med.	= medium	temp.	= temperature
min.	= minutes	veg.	= vegetable

KEFTETHAKIA

1½ lb. ground beef
1 egg
1 T. minced parsley
1 onion, grated
1 c. dry bread crumbs
1 T. chopped fresh mint
¼ t. cinnamon
1 t. salt
grinding pepper

combine these 9 ingred.
let stand ½ hr.
shape into walnut sized balls
dust lightly with flour
saute until browned on all sides

serve on toothpicks

serves: 8

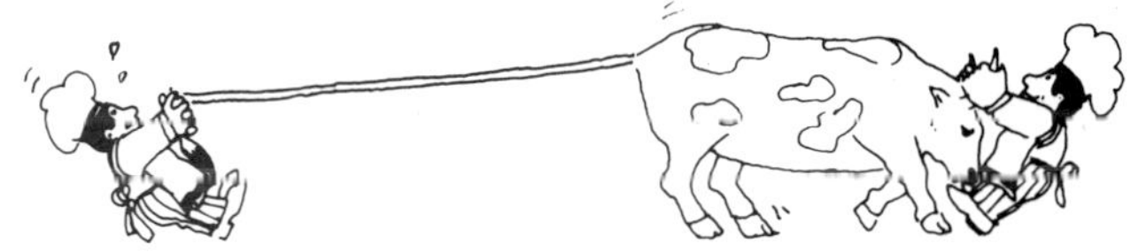

1 lb. ground beef
1 egg
½ t. gr. coriander
⅛ t. ginger
⅛ t. cloves
⅛ t. cinnamon
¾ t. curry pd.
1 T. instant minced onion
½ t. instant minced garlic
1 t. salt
grinding pepper

combine these 11 ingred.
shape into bite-sized balls
saute until browned on
all sides

1 lg. can button mushrooms, drained

add to meat balls
heat
serve mushroom and meatball on cocktail pick

chutney or
chili sauce

serve sauce as dip

serves: 6-8

1 lb. chicken livers
½ c. minced onion
½ c. minced celery
2 T. margarine

} saute these 3 ingred. in margarine
until liver is light pink
chop very fine or put in blender

2 hard-cooked eggs, chopped
¼ t. dry mustard
⅛ t. nutmeg
½ t. M.S.G.
2 T. brandy (preservative)
¾ t. salt
grinding pepper

} mix in these 7 ingred.
store refrigerated

crackers
french bread

} serve on your choice

serves: 4-6

CHOPPED LIVER DELUXE

¾ lb. calves liver
2 T. margarine

} saute liver until light pink
chop finely with a knife

1 med. onion grated
1 hard-boiled egg, chopped
½ t. salt
grinding pepper

} mix in these 4 ingred.

mayonnaise

} add enough mayonnaise to make
a smooth consistency

sieved egg yolk

} sprinkle yolk over top to garnish

bread rounds or crackers

} serve with bread or crackers

serves: 4-6

2½ c. water
1¾ c. white vinegar
2 T. peppercorns
1½ T. whole allspice
2 T. sugar
1½ t. salt

combine these 6 ingred.
simmer 10 min.

1 onion
½ green pepper
½ red pepper
1½ lb. knockwurst, ½" slices

slice these 3 vegetables in rings
layer with knockwurst in bowl
pour liquid over top
marinate 3 days or more

will keep for several weeks

serves: 4-6

HAYSTACKS

1 onion, minced
1 stalk celery, minced
3 T. margarine
} gently saute onion and celery in margarine until soft

2 c. sauerkraut, squeezed dry
1 c. minced cooked ham
½ c. chicken bouillon
} add these 3 ingred.
simmer until liquid is almost evaporated

¼ c. flour
} sprinkle flour over top
stir while cooking until thickened
shape into bite-sized balls

1 c. cracker crumbs
} roll in crumbs to coat well

deep fat 365°
} deep fry until golden
drain on paper towels

chili sauce
} serve hot with chili sauce

serves: 8

JAMBON BOATS

¾ pkg. Danish ham slices, minced
¼ c. chopped walnuts
¼ c. minced celery
4 T. drained crushed pineapple
½ c. mayonnaise
1 t. lemon juice
½ t. salt

} combine these 7 ingred.

30 - 2" pieces celery

} fill celery with mix

refrigerate covered until ready to serve

30 pieces

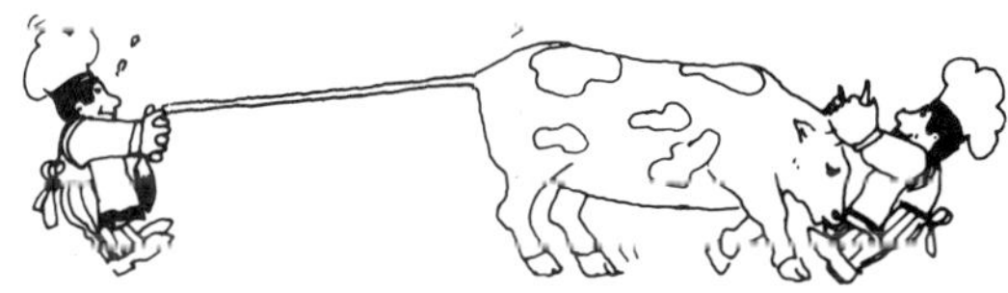

ASPARAGUS UNDER COVER

1 c. biscuit mix
¼ t. Fines Herbes
1/3 c. milk

} combine these 3 ingred.
with a fork until
dough is stiff and slightly sticky
knead on floured board
until smooth
roll out ⅛" thick cut 6 4x2½" strips of dough

12 cooked asparagus spears
6 slices Danish ham
mustard

} lay 2 asparagus spears and 1 slice of ham
on each strip of dough
spread with mustard
roll up
lay seam down on greased baking sheet

bake 400° for 8-10 min.

prepared cheese sauce

} heat sauce
serve over top

makes 6 rolls

CHERRY-O-CHICKEN 25

30 cherry tomatoes	} scoop out pulp leaving shell intact
1 can boned chicken 3 oz. cream cheese 3 T. mayonnaise dash garlic salt ½ t. salt dash white pepper	} combine these 6 ingred. until smooth stuff tomato shells
sesame seeds	} top with seeds
parsley	} garnish with parsley

makes 30 tomatoes

RUMAKI

¼ lb. calves liver, cut 1" cubes
1 onion, sliced
¼ t. salt
2 T. margarine

combine these 4 ingred.
saute until liver is light pink about 2 min.

8 slices bacon, cut in half
16 water chestnuts

wrap 1 piece liver and 1 water chestnut
in 1 strip of bacon
secure with toothpick

10 min. before serving
saute until bacon is crispy on all sides

serves: 6

8 slices bacon, cut strip in half
16 1" chunks pickled watermelon rind
8 water chestnuts, cut in half

wrap each strip bacon around 1 watermelon
and 1 water chestnut
secure with toothpick

10 min. before serving
saute until bacon is done on all sides

serves: 4-6

BRUSSEL SURPRISES

brussels sprouts

} plan on 3 halves per person
cut brussels in half through core
cut out the heart of each half

stuffed olives
ripe olives
cocktail onions
water chestnuts

} insert your choice of one in each half

bacon strips

} wrap each half in strip of bacon
secure with picks

saute until bacon is done on all sides

bananas   } peel bananas
                                            cut into 1" pieces

soft peanut butter   } coat with peanut butter
granola or other natural cereal   roll in cereal

slice

serve with picks

FLAVOR BARRELS

7 oz. can tuna, drained
4 oz. cream cheese
1 T. mayonnaise
1 T. lemon juice
1T. chopped pickles
dash celery salt
½ t. salt
dash white pepper

} combine these 8 ingred.

2 lg. cucumbers

} cut off each end of cucumber
with carrot peeler, dig out seeds to make a barrel
stuff with tuna filling

chill well

slice thin circles

cracker rounds

} serve on crackers

serves: 8

2 c. grated yellow cheese
¾ c. milk
½ t. worcestershire sauce
2 drops tabasco sauce
¼ t. mustard pd.
¾ c. mayonnaise

} combine these 6 ingred.
gently heat to melt cheese
refrig. several hrs. or longer

crackers or
raw vegetables

} serve with your choice

makes 2 cups

WAFER WONDERS

½ c. grated yellow cheese
1/3 c. blue cheese
¾ c. margarine

} cream together these 3 ingredients

½ clove garlic, minced
1 T. minced parsley
2 T. minced green onion
½ t. cumin or
   chili pd. or
    mustard pd.
2 c. flour

} mix in these 5 ingred.
shape into 1½" thick rolls
wrap in wax paper

chill well

slice ¼" slices
place on greased sheet
bake 350° for 8 to 10 min.

1 onion, chopped
1 T. margarine

} saute onions 3 min.

1 lb. asparagus
1 c. water
½ t. salt

} add these 3 ingred.
cover
cook 15 min.
puree in blender

1 c. diced ham
2 c. milk

} add these 2 ingred.
heat very gently a few min.

serves: 4

 GREEN SUPREME

1 bunch broccoli — } blanch broccoli in boiling salted water 5 min.
drain
put into blender

1 can cond. cream of chicken soup
½ can milk
1 T. instant minced onion
¼ t. garlic salt
¼ red bell pepper or pimiento, minced — } add these 5 ingred.
puree only until green and red flecks are visible

serve hot or cold

serves: 4-6

1 onion, sliced
2 T. margarine

} very gently saute onions 4 min.

1 small cauliflower, separated
¼ c. water
1/3 t. salt

} add these 3 ingred.
cover
simmer 6 min.
puree

2 c. rich chicken broth
½ c. milk
season to taste

} mix in these 3 ingred.
heat to serving temp.

½ c. sour cream

} stir in cream

serves: 4-6

DANISH DILLY SOUP

<table>
<tr><td>2 cucumbers, peeled, sliced
½ c. chopped green onion
1 bay leaf
2 T. margarine</td><td>} gently saute these 4 ingred. 10 min.</td></tr>
<tr><td>1½ T. flour</td><td>} grad. blend in flour</td></tr>
<tr><td>2½ c. rich chicken broth
salt to taste</td><td>} add these 2 ingred.
simmer 20 min.
puree smooth</td></tr>
<tr><td>1 t. minced dill weed
¼ c. condensed milk or cream
¾ c. milk</td><td>} stir in these 3 ingred.
chill well</td></tr>
<tr><td>lemon slices</td><td>} garnish soup</td></tr>
</table>

serves: 4

2½ c. minced celery
¾ c. water
¼ t. salt
} combine these 3 ingred.
simmer 5 min.

¼ c. chopped green onion
1 can cond. cream of chicken soup
} add these 2 ingred.
puree only until celery is coarsely chopped

¼ to ½ c. milk
} add milk to desired consistency

heat to serving temp.

serves: 4

ONION SOUP EXTRAORDINAIRE

3 T. veg. oil
2 onions, sliced
¼ t. salt
grinding pepper

} saute onions very gently 15 min.
do not brown

1 t. flour

} sprinkle flour over top
stir in

2 cans beef bouillon
2 cans water
½ c. dry vermouth
2 beef bouillon cubes

} add these 4 ingred.
simmer uncovered 25 min.
fill 6 individual soup bowls

6 slices stale French bread
margarine
Parmesan cheese

} top bread with margarine and parmesan
top each bowl with a slice
broil few min. to melt cheese

serves: 6

HEARTY POTATO SOUP 39

4 meaty hamhocks
5 c. water

} simmer ham 45 min.

3 potatoes, diced
3 T. instant minced onion
¼ t. mace or cumin
1½ t. salt

} add these 4 ingred.
cover
simmer 20 min.

1 lb. can cream-style corn
2 c. milk
taste for seasoning

} add these 3 ingred.
reheat to serving temp.

serves: 4

GARDEN PUREE SOUP

3 carrots, scraped, diced
2 stalks celery, chopped
1 onion, chopped
1 T. margarine

> combine these 3 vegetables
> reserve ¼ veg.
> saute remaining 3 min.

1 c. chicken broth

> add broth
> cover
> cook 4 min.
> puree
> return to pan

3 c. chicken broth
¼ c. dry vermouth
1½ t. sugar
¼ t. garlic salt
½ t. salt - to taste
grinding pepper

> add these 6 ingred.
> along with reserved veg.
> simmer 5 min.

chopped parsley

> sprinkle with parsley to serve

serves: 6

1 bunch broccoli, chopped   } blanch broccoli in boiling salted water for 5 min.
drain off all but 1 c. water

4 chicken bouillon cubes   } add bouillon
puree smooth

1½ c. milk
½ pkg. frozen peas
½ can water chestnuts, diced   } add these 3 ingred.
heat only until peas are hot

serves: 4-6

SUPER SUPPER SOUP

1 onion, chopped
½ c. chopped green onion
2 cloves garlic, smashed
2 T. veg. oil

} saute these 4 ingred. 5 min.

2 tomatoes, chopped
3 T. soy sauce
2-3 drops tabasco sauce
6 c. beef broth

} add these 4 ingred.
cover
simmer ½ hr.

1 lb. gr. beef
¼ c. minced onions
1 egg
2 t. sesame seeds
¼ t. ginger
1 t. salt
grinding pepper

} combine these 7 ingred.
shape into 1" balls
drop into hot soup
simmer 20 min.

1 c. fine noodles

} add noodles   simmer 10 min.

(continued next page)

1 egg white
1 t. water

} beat egg white until frothy
fry gently to make an omelet
roll up
cut in narrow strips to serve in soup

serves: 6-8

SOUP CARIBBEAN

1 can cond. bean soup
1 can cond. tomato soup
2 cans water
1 T. instant minced onion
1 T. worchestershire sauce

} combine these 5 ingred.
heat to simmer

crackers or croutons

} serve with your choice

serves: 4

SOUPE ALBONDIGAS

1 lb. ground beef
2 T. instant minced onion
¾ c. bread crumbs
½ c. pine nuts if available
1 egg
¾ t. chili pd.
¼ t. cumin
1 t. salt

combine these 8 ingred.
shape into 1" meatballs

1½ qt. rich beef bouillon

bring broth to a simmer
add meatballs
simmer 10 min.

serves: 6

AVGOLEMONO

1 can Campbell's chicken broth
1 can College Inn chicken broth
½ c. minute rice

} combine these 3 ingred.
cook 3 min.

3 egg whites, beaten stiff
3 egg yolks, beaten
juice of 1 small lemon

} combine these 3 ingred.
add ¼ c. hot soup to egg
grad. add this to soup
stirring constantly
heat without boiling

serves: 4

CHICKEN HOT POT

4 c. chicken broth
salt to taste
1 chicken, cut up

} simmer chicken 45 min.

3 carrots, diced
2 leeks or 4 green onions, sliced
1 t. celery salt
½ t. M.S.G.
½ t. garlic salt
¼ t. seasoned pepper

} add these 6 ingred.
simmer 20 min.

1½ c. egg noodles

} add noodles
simmer until tender

serves: 4-6

5 c. water
¾ c. white beans

} combine these 2 ingred.
simmer 1 hr. or til beans tender

5 c. water
8 chicken bouillon cubes
1 onion
5 green onions
2 carrots
3 stalks celery
2 potatoes
1/3 c. rice
1 c. corn
1 c. peas
1 bay leaf
½ t. tarragon

dice vegetables
add these 12 ingred.
cover
simmer 45 min.

serves: 4

PEANUT SOUP

1 onion, chopped
2 stalks celery, chopped
¼ c. uncooked rice
¼ t. salt
1 T. margarine

} combine these 5 ingred.
gently saute 5 min.

3 c. chicken bouillon
1 bay leaf
1 small dried hot red chili or
few drops tabasco sauce

} add these 3 ingred.
cover
simmer 15 min.
remove bay leaf and chili

½ c. peanut butter

} mix in peanut butter

¼ c. sour cream

} just before serving
blend in sour cream

serves: 4

1 13 oz. can clear consomme madrilene
1 pkg. unflavored gelatin
} sprinkle gelatin over ½ c. consomme
to soften
heat very gently to dissolve
add to remaining consomme

1 T. lemon juice
¼ c. minced celery
1 green onion, chopped
1 12 oz. can sliced beets and juice
} add these 4 ingred.
put in mold
refrigerate until set
unmold

1 c. mayonnaise
1½ T. prepared horseradish
} combine these 2 ingred.
serve with salad

serves: 4

ORANGE CARNIVAL

¼ c. raisins
2 T. cointreau or orange flavored
   liqueur

} combine these 2 ingred.
macerate ½ hr.

2 c. grated carrots
1 c. orange juice
⅛ t. cayenne pepper
⅛ t. ginger
½ t. salt

} combine these 5 ingred.
chill well

lettuce leaves

} line salad bowls
divide carrot mixture on each
drain and top with raisins

serves: 4

1 lg. eggplant

} bake whole eggplant at 400° for 1 hr.
peel off skin
chop pulp

½ c. chopped green onion
¼ c. chopped green pepper
2 tomatoes, peeled, chopped
¼ t. garlic pd.
1½ t. seasoned salt

} add these 5 ingred.
serve warm or chilled

serves: 4-6

CUCUMBER CRESENTS

2 med. cucumbers

peel cucumbers
cut ½ lengthwise
dig out seeds
cut ¼" thick slices

½ c. chopped green onion
1 T. soy sauce
1 T. vinegar
1 T. lemon juice
1 T. sugar
1 T. sesame seed oil or veg. oil
dash tabasco sauce
½ t. salt

combine these 8 ingred. in jar
shake well
add cucumbers
chill several hrs. shaking frequently

lettuce

serve on bed of lettuce

serves: 4

2 pkg. frozen peas, thawed
1/3 c. minced celery
1/3 c. chopped green onion
2 T. minced fresh mint
    or ½ t. dried mint
½ c. herbed vinegar
2 T. water
1/3 c. veg. oil
¾ t. salt

combine all ingred.
marinate overnight

lettuce leaves

serve on lettuce

serves: 6

SPINACH BLAZE

6 strips bacon, diced
4 green onions, chopped

> cook till bacon is ½ done
> add onions
> continue to cook til done

juice of 1 lemon
dash worcestershire sauce
¼ c. red wine vinegar
2 T. sugar
¼ t. salt

> add these 5 ingred.

1 lg. bunch spinach

> put clean spinach into salad bowl
> toss with dressing to bruise leaves

3 T. cognac or brandy

> heat cognac
> ignite
> gradually pour flaming cognac over salad
> toss to blend in
> serve immediately

serves: 4

1 small head lettuce, shredded
2 oranges, sectioned
1/3 c. sliced ripe olives
2 carrots, sliced in circles
roquefort cheese, crumbled

} combine these 5 ingred.

spicy french dressing

} toss with dressing

serves: 4-6

SPINACH THE GOURMET WAY

2 slices bacon, diced	} saute bacon until half done
½ lb. mushrooms, sliced 1 T. butter ¼ t. seasoned salt	} add these 3 ingred. cook until bacon crisp
1 T. lemon juice	} add lemon
1 lg. bunch spinach, chopped	} put spinach in salad bowl toss with dressing bruising leaves
¾ c. shredded cheddar cheese	} toss in cheese

serves: 4-6

1 c. mandarin orange sections
1 c. minature marshmellows
1 c. pineapple chunks   } combine these 5 ingred.
1 c. shredded coconut
1 c. sour cream

chill for 24 hours

CRANNY WALDORF

½ c. cranberry sauce
½ c. veg. oil
3 T. lemon juice
½ t. paprika
½ t. salt

combine these 5 ingred.
puree smooth

½ c. chopped green onion
¾ c. chopped celery
½ c. chopped walnuts
2 to 3 apples, diced

combine these 4 ingred.
toss with dressing
may keep refrigerated for several hrs.

lettuce leaves

serve on lettuce

serves: 4-6

CHICKEN CELESTIAL

2 c. cooked chicken, cubed
2 stalks celery, chopped
½ green pepper chopped
10 stuffed olives, sliced
1 tomato, cubed
1 c. pineapple chunks
½ c. chopped walnuts
2 t. instant minced onions
dash worchestershire sauce
salt to taste
½ c. mayonnaise

} combine these 11 ingred.

chill several hrs.

serves: 4

CHICKEN ELEGANCE

1 pkg. unflavored gelatin
¼ c. cold water
} sprinkle gelatin over water
let stand 5 min.
dissolve over hot water

2 c. whole cranberry sauce
1 c. crushed drained pineapple
} combine these 2 ingred. with gelatin
pour into 10x6x1½" cake pan
chill until firm

1 pkg. unflavored gelatin
¼ c. cold water
} sprinkle gelatin over water
dissolve over hot water

1 c. mayonnaise
3 T. lemon juice
2 c. diced cooked chicken
¾ c. chopped celery
¼ c. chopped green onion
2 T. minced parsley
¾ t. salt
} stir in these 7 ingred.
pour over cranberry layer
chill til set

serves: 6

1 pkg. frozen peas, thawed
1¾ c. diced cooked ham
½ c. sliced celery
1/3 c. mayonnaise

} combine these 4 ingred.

toasted almonds (opt.)
2 hard-boiled eggs, sliced

} garnish to serve

lettuce leaves

} serve on lettuce

serves: 4

HAM TROPICAL

2 c. cooked ham, sliced julienne
½ c. diced celery
2/3 c. pineapple chunks
1 T. chopped pickles
a few chopped dates or raisins

} combine these 5 ingred.

2 T. mayonnaise
1 T. french dressing
1 T. prepared mustard

} combine these 3 ingred.
toss with salad
chill

1 banana, sliced
1/3 coconut

} garnish to serve

serves: 4

1 lg. bunch fresh spinach
¼ c. mayonnaise
} toss spinach with mayonnaise

1 pkg. Swiss cheese
1 pkg. Danish ham
} slice cheese and ham in julienne strip
toss with salad

2 hard-boiled eggs, sliced
1 tomato, cut in wedges
} garnish with eggs and tomatoes

serves: 4

GOURMET'S DELIGHT

2 sweet potatoes, cooked, diced 1 c. drained pineapple chunks 1 lg. banana, sliced ¾ c. sliced celery ¾ c. cooked ham or chicken, diced	} combine these 5 ingred.
3 T. mayonnaise	} stir in mayonnaise
lettuce leaves	} serve on lettuce
radish roses parsley sprigs	} garnish

serves: 6

1 bunch green onions, chopped
2 slices bacon, diced
¼ t. garlic salt

} saute these 3 ingred. until bacon is crisp
reserve

1 can string beans, drained
¼ c. wine vinegar

} add these 2 ingred. to pan
heat to serving temp.

¼ c. mayonnaise
¼ c. sour cream

} mix in these 2 ingred.
top with reserved mixture

serves: 4-6

GREEN BEANS ORIENTAL

3 slices bacon, diced   } saute bacon til crisp / remove and reserve bacon

2 t. instant minced onion
2 T. wine vinegar
1 T. sugar
½ t. salt

} stir these 4 ingred. into pan

1 lb. can green beans, drained
1 lb. can bean sprouts, drained

} add these 2 vegetables / heat only to serving temp.

top with reserved bacon

serves: 4

MISTY JADE

1 pkg. frozen broccoli	} cook broccoli as pkg. directs
1 c. mashed potatoes 1 t. lemon juice ¼ t. celery salt ⅛ t. garlic salt ½ t. seasoned salt ¼ t. salt	} combine these 6 ingred. with broccoli in blender puree pile in greased casserole
¼ c. cracker crumbs ¼ c. parmesan cheese	} sprinkle crumbs and cheese over

bake 350° for 15 min.

serves: 4

BRUSSELS SWEET-SOUR

1½ lb. brussels sprouts } blanch brussels in boiling
salted water 5 min.
drain

3 T. margarine
1 onion, minced } saute onions 7 min.

¼ c. flour } sprinkle flour over top
stir in

2 c. beef bouillon
dash cloves
salt to taste
pepper } grad. stir in these 4 ingred.
cook til smooth and thickened

2 T. brown sugar
2 T. vinegar or lemon juice } add these 2 ingred.
taste for flavor balance

stir in brussels
heat to serving temp.   serves: 4-6

4 lb. cabbage, shredded
½ c. beef bouillon
3 T. instant minced onion
1 bay leaf
3 cloves
1 clove garlic, mashed
1 t. salt
grinding pepper

} combine these 8 ingred.
cover
cook 10 min.

2 c. white sauce
1 T. curry pd.

} mix in these 2 ingred.
transfer into casserole

¼ c. cracker crumbs
¼ c. parmesan cheese

} sprinkle these 2 ingred. over top
bake 400° for 15 min.

serves: 4-6

CAULIFLOWER HONGROISE

1 cauliflower, separated } blanch cauliflower in boiling salted water 5 min.
drain

1 onion, minced
2 T. margarine } saute onion 3 min.

1 T. paprika
2 t. flour } stir in these 2 ingred.

1 c. chicken broth } grad. stir in broth   cook smooth

1½ tomatoes, chopped
1 bay leaf
½ t. salt
grinding pepper } add these 4 ingred.
simmer 15 min.
uncover
simmer to reduce liquid

2 T. cream
1½ T. lemon juice } add these 2 ingred.

serves: 4-6

2 onions, chopped
¾ T. curry pd.
¼ t. salt
2 T. margarine

} combine these 4 ingred.
saute 5 min.

1 c. chicken broth

} add broth
simmer 10 min.

1 cauliflower, separated

} add cauliflower
cover
cook 6 min.
uncover
simmer to reduce liquid

serves: 4-6

BOMBAY EGGPLANT

4 small eggplant } slit open lengthwise on one side only
scoop out portions of insides

1 onion, chopped
2 T. margarine } saute onion 3 min.

1½ T. flour
1½ t. curry pd. } blend in these 2 ingred.

2 T. chutney
1 T. lemon juice
3 T. apple sauce
½ c. bouillon
½ t. salt } grad. blend in these 5 ingred.
cook until thickened
stuff eggplant
lay in baking dish

¼ c. water } add water to dish
cover
bake 350° for ½ hr.

serves: 4

2½ c. white sauce
1-2 t. curry pd.
½ t. worcestershire sauce
2 c. diced cooked chicken
insides of onion, chopped (see below)

} combine these 5 ingred.

4 lg. onions

} boil onions 25 min. drain
gently cut out insides of onions to make cups
fill cups with chicken mixture
transfer to casserole
cover
bake 350° for 25 min.

pimiento
parsley

} garnish to serve

serves: 4

PISELLI E PASTA

2 T. margarine
4 slices bacon, diced
1½ c. chopped onions
⅛ t. sugar
½ t. salt

combine these 5 ingred.
saute gently 20 min.

1 pkg. frozen peas
2 T. concentrated beef bouillon

add peas and bouillon
heat only until thawed

1 lb. noodles, cooked, drained
½ c. Parmesan cheese or
   Romano cheese

toss together noodles and cheese

add ½ of pea mixture
toss
transfer to serving dish
pour remainder pea mixture over top

serves: 6

PRIMAVERA DELUXE

2 T. olive oil
2 slices bacon, diced
1 lg. onion, chopped
1 clove garlic, smashed

} saute these 4 ingred. 20 min.

4 oz. jar chopped pimiento
1 c. uncooked rice
¼ t. saffron
2 c. chicken bouillon

} add these 4 ingred.
cover
simmer 20 min.

1 pkg. frozen peas, thawed
1 pkg. cut asparagus, thawed

} stir in peas   transfer to casserole
top with asparagus   cover
bake 350° for 10 to 15 min.

serves: 4-5

CURRIED POTATO BAKE

1 onion, chopped
5 T. margarine

} saute onions 5 min.

5 T. flour

} grad. stir in flour

2 T. tomato paste
1½ t. curry pd.
pinch basil
grinding pepper
2½ c. chicken bouillon

} grad stir in these 5 ingred.
stir until thickened and smooth

4 boiled potatoes, diced

} add potatoes
transfer to casserole

bake 350° for 30 min.

serves: 4-6

POTATO STRATA BAKE

4 baked potatoes } scoop out insides of potato leaving shell intact

1 c. cottage cheese
3 T. milk
¾ t. seasoned salt } add these 3 ingred. to hot potato beat smooth

sliced cheddar cheese } stuff shells alternately with potato mixture and cheese

bake 400° for 10 min.

serves: 4

MOM'S GERMAN POTATOES

2 slices bacon, diced
1 onion, minced } fry bacon & onions 10 min.

2 T. margarine
2 T. flour } stir in these 2 ingred.

¾ c. water
¼ t. sugar
¼ c. vinegar
salt to taste } grad. stir in these 4 ingred.
cook smooth and thickened

4 to 6 potatoes } cook & slice potatoes
mix with sauce

serves: 4 to 6

8 slices bacon, diced
2 onions, chopped

} saute onions and bacon until bacon is done
drain off fat

1 #2½ can sauerkraut and juice
1 #2½ can tomatoes and juice
½ c. brown sugar

} add these 3 ingred.
transfer to casserole

bake uncovered   350° for 1 hr.

serves: 8

RICE N GREEN CASSEROLE

2 green onions, chopped
1 clove garlic, smashed
2 t. butter
3 c. chicken bouillon

} combine these 4 ingred.
bring to boil

1½ c. rice

} add rice
cover
simmer 15 min.

2 bunches spinach, chopped

} add spinach
cook 10 min. longer
transfer to casserole

½ c. Parmesan cheese

} sprinkle cheese over top

bake uncovered 350° for 10 min.

serves: 6

COINTREAU ACCENT

4 sweet potatoes

} cook potatoes in boiling salted water until tender
drain   peel   mash

2 ripe bananas, sliced
4 T. Cointreau liqueur
4 T. margarine
1 t. salt
grinding pepper

} blend in these 5 ingred.
transfer to casserole
bake 350° for 25 min.

serves: 4-6

SWEET POTATO FRY

3 med. sweet potatoes, peeled
2 med. onions

} slice potatoes and onions ⅛" thick into pan

4 T. bacon fat
1 T. margarine
¾ t. salt
grinding pepper

} add these 4 ingred.
saute gently until under side is crisp
turn   cook until crisp

¾ c. sour cream

} gently stir in sour cream

cook 3 min.

serves: 4

6 yams or sweet potatoes   } boil yams in salted water til tender
                             drain   peel   mash

1 sm. can concentrated orange juice
1 cube margarine   } add these 3 ingred.
2 T. dry sherry   pile in casserole

bake 350° to serving temp.
about 15 min.

serves: 6-8

SQUASH SUPREME

3 c. cooked mashed yellow squash
1 c. sour cream
1 can cond. cream of chicken soup   combine these 5 ingred.
1 T. grated onion
1 grated carrot

1 pkg. herb bread dressing   layer ¾ dressing in greased baking dish
top with squash
top with remaining dressing

bake 350° for ½ hr.

serves: 4-6

ZUCCHINI ORIENT

6 med. zucchini, quartered lengthwise
¼ c. bacon fat
½ t. salt
grinding pepper

} combine these 4 ingred.
saute 5 min.
transfer to serving dish

3 T. vinegar
1 T. sugar
½ clove garlic, smashed

} add these 3 ingred. to pan
simmer 2 min.
pour over zucchini

serves: 4-6

MARDI GRAS CREOLE

½ c. chopped green peppers
1 lg. onion, chopped
1 clove garlic, smashed
2 T. olive oil

} combine these 4 ingred.
saute 5 min.

3 T. flour

} blend in flour

2 c. beef bouillon

} grad. blend in bouillon

1 c. chopped mushrooms
2 chopped peeled tomatoes
6 unpeeled zucchini, sliced
¼ c. chopped ripe olives
2 T. white wine

} add these 5 ingred.
simmer 15 min.

serves: 6

1 onion, chopped
1 clove garlic, smashed
1 c. rice
2 T. margarine

saute these 4 ingred. 8 min.
stirring constantly

4 oz. can (ortegas) chopped chilies
3 tomatoes, chopped
4 oz. can mushrooms & stock
1½ c. beef or chicken bouillon

add these 4 ingred.
cover
simmer 20 min.
uncover
simmer until liquid is evaporated

serves: 4

 RICE SAFFRON

1 onion, minced
1 stalk celery, minced
½ bay leaf
pinch saffron
1 c. rice
2 T. margarine

saute these 6 ingred. 5 min.
stirring

2 c. chicken bouillon

add bouillon
cover
simmer 20 min.
let stand covered 10 min.

serves: 4

¼ lb. ham, diced
2 T. margarine

} brown ham stirring constantly

6 mushrooms, sliced
3 green onions, chopped

} add these 2 ingred.
saute 1 min.

2 c. cooked rice
2 eggs, beaten lightly
2 T. soy sauce
¼ t. salt
grinding pepper

} stir in these 5 ingred.
stir-fry until egg is set

serves: 3-4

CALAS

1 c. rice | cook rice 40 min.
2½ c. water | puree cooked rice in blender
½ t. salt | ¼ c. at a time until half pureed

1 pkg. yeast | combine yeast and water 5 min.
½ c. warm water | add to rice   cover   let rise 12 hrs.

2 eggs
¼ c. honey
1½ c. flour | beat in these 5 ingred.
¼ t. nutmeg | let stand 45 min.
¾ t. salt

deep fat 360° | drop 1 T. of batter at a time into hot veg. oil
| deep fry until browned on all sides
| drain on absorbent paper

serves: 6

Variations:
raisin-nut   coconut | blend in your favorite flavor
cinnamon-sugar   peanut butter | deep fry as above

1 onion, chopped
1 T. veg. oil

} saute onions 5 min.

2 c. cooked rice
1 c. diced cooked beef
1 jar sliced mushrooms, drained
1 can water chestnuts, sliced
3 eggs, beaten

} add these 5 ingred.
stir fry until eggs are set

soy sauce

} serve with soy sauce

serves: 4

NOODLES ROYALE

4½ c. noodles } cook noodles as pkg. directs
drain

1 onion, minced
4 T. margarine } saute onions 4 min.

2 T. flour } blend in flour

2 c. milk
1½ t. worcestershire sauce
¼ t. salt } grad. stir in these 3 ingred.
cook until smooth and thickened
toss with noodles

½ pkg. boiled ham, cut in strips
4 slices Swiss cheese, cut in strips } toss in cheese and ham
transfer to serving dish

paprika
margarine } top with paprika & margarine

serves: 6-8

BEAN THREAD NOODLES

1 pkg. thread noodles

} soak noodles in warm water ½ hr.
drain

1 c. beef bouillon
1 c. chicken bouillon
2 T. soy sauce
dash garlic pd.
1 can sliced mushrooms & liquid

} combine these 5 ingred. with noodles
cook until noodles tender
drain to serve

serves: 6

CRAN-APPLE POULTRY STUFFING

2 c. cranberries, chopped
2 apples, chopped
8 c. dried bread, crumbled

combine these 3 ingred.

2 onions, chopped
1 clove garlic, smashed
4 stalks celery, chopped
¼ c. margarine

saute these 4 ingred. 5 min.

3 T. chopped parsley
2 t. poultry seasoning
1 t. sage
¼ t. tabasco sauce
¼ t. salt - to taste
2 ½ c. chicken bouillon

add these 6 ingred.
along with bread
toss to mix
stuff poultry

4 firm pears

} core & peel pears
lay halves in baking dish

¼ c. water
¼ c. honey
2 T. lemon juice
½ t. ginger

} combine these 4 ingred. in pan
simmer 5 min.
pour over pears

bake 350° for 15 min.
basting with juice frequently

serves: 4

SUGAR N' SPICE

½ c. pineapple juice
½ c. vinegar
1¼ c. sugar
1 cinnamon stick
1 t. whole cloves
½ t. whole allspice

combine these 6 ingred. in pan
simmer 5 min.

1 lb. mixed dried fruit

add fruit
cover
refrig. several days

serve beside meat or poultry

serves: 6

GOULASH VIENNESE

2 c. chopped onion
3 T. veg. oil
} saute onions 5 min.

½ lb. mushrooms, sliced
3 lbs. beef stew, cubed
1 T. caraway seeds
½ t. marjoram
2 cloves garlic, smashed
1 T. salt
2 beef bouillon cubes
} add these 7 ingred.
saute stirring to brown meat

1½ c. water
¼ c. catsup
½ c. tomato paste
2 T. paprika
} add these 4 ingred.
cover
simmer until meat is tender

serves: 6

HOT POT DELUXE

1 onion, chopped
1 clove garlic, smashed
2 T. veg. oil

} saute these 3 ingred. 5 min.
transfer to casserole

2 lbs. beef stew, cubed
¼ c. flour
1 t. salt

} combine these 3 ingred. in bag shake to coat
brown meat in pan
transfer to casserole

1 c. beef bouillon
1 c. red wine
1½ t. worcestershire sauce
½ t. oregano
¼ t. salt
grinding pepper

} combine these 6 ingred. in pan
scrape pan well
pour over casserole

3 potatoes, diced
12 small onions
1 can water chestnuts, sliced
1 can button mushrooms, drained
salt

} transfer these 4 ingred. to casserole
sprinkle top with salt
cover
bake 350° for 1 hr.

serves: 6

SOUTH SEA SIMMER

2 lb. stew meat, 1" cubes
1 c. chopped onion
1 T. salt
grinding pepper
3 T. veg. oil

} combine these 5 ingred. in pan
cook til meat is browned

¾ c. beef bouillon

} add bouillon   cover   simmer 1 hr.

2 bananas, sliced

} add bananas
simmer 5 min.

hot cooked rice

} serve with rice

toasted almonds

} top with almonds

serves: 4-6

BOEUF VIN BLANC

2 onions, sliced
2 T. veg. oil
} saute onions slowly 10 min.
reserve onions

2 lb. round steak, cut 1" cubes
½ c. flour
1 t. paprika
¼ t. M.S.G.
1 t. salt
grinding pepper
} combine these 6 ingred. in bag
shake to coat meat

2 T. veg. oil } add oil to pan   brown meat on all sides

1 c. dry white wine } add wine along with reserved onions
cover   simmer ½ hr.
uncover   simmer to reduce liquid

½ lb. mushrooms, sliced
2 T. margarine
dash salt
} saute mushrooms 4 min.
arrange beef on platter
top with mushrooms

cooked rice } serve with rice   serves: 4

SWISS STEAK A LA BOURGEOISE

1½ lb. round steak, tenderized
1 T. veg. oil

} brown steak on both sides in oil
transfer to baking dish

1 can cond. onion soup
½ soup can water
4 carrots, pare, cut 2" pieces
4 potatoes, cubed
2 stalks celery, sliced
½ green pepper, cut strips
taste for salt

add these 7 ingred.
cover
bake 350° for 1¼ hr.
uncover
bake 10 min.

2 T. chopped parsley

} sprinkle parsley over

serves: 4

 BEEF BURMESE STYLE

3 c. chopped onion
3 cloves garlic
2 t. ginger root or ½ t. pd. ginger
1 t. lemon juice
¾ t. chili pd.
2 t. salt
½ c. veg. oil
} pound these 7 ingred. to paste
or puree in blender to make marinade

3 lb. top round or sirloin
} cut meat in 1" cubes
marinate ½ day or longer

2 T. veg. oil
} heat oil   remove meat from marinade & brown

4 tomatoes, seeded, sliced
1 c. water
2 beef bouillon cubes
} add these 3 ingred. along with marinade
cover
simmer 1 hr.

rice or noodles
} serve with rice or noodles

serves: 8-10

2 onions, chopped
2 T. veg. oil
} saute onions 5 min.

¾ lb. fresh mushrooms, sliced
2 T. margarine
} add these 2 ingred.   saute 4 min.
reserve this mixture

2½ lb. top round, 2" long thick strips } brown meat in pan

2 bouillon
2 t. worcestershire sauce
1 T. soy sauce
½ c. tomato sauce
salt to taste
} add these 5 ingred.
along with onion mixture
cover
simmer 45 min.

1 c. sour cream or yogurt } stir in sour cream   serves: 6

hot cooked rice } serve with rice

ITALIAN ROULADE

2 2½ lb. ea. round steaks
1 t. dry spaghetti sauce mix } combine seasonings
1 t. salt   pound into steaks
grinding pepper

2 slices bacon, diced
1 onion, minced } saute these 2 ingred. til bacon done

¼ c. pimiento stuffed olives, chopped } add these 2 ingred.   spoon ½ down center of each steak
2 c. Ricotta cheese   roll steaks jelly roll fashion   tie with string

2 T. flour
½ t. salt } sprinkle these 3 ingred. on rolls.
grinding pepper   brown on all sides in pan

8 oz. tomato sauce } combine & add these 3 ingred.   pour over rolls
½ c. water   cover
remainder spaghetti sauce mix   simmer 1½ hr. til tender   remove strings

serve topped with sauce   serves: 6-8

INDONESIA MELANGE

2½ lb. round steak, 2" pieces
½ c. flour
1 t. salt
grinding pepper

} combine these 4 ingred. in bag
shake to coat meat

3 T. veg. oil
1 clove garlic, smashed
1 onion, chopped

} brown meat with these 3 ingred.

1 can beef broth
1½ t. curry pd.
½ t. ginger
¼ c. raisins
½ c. chutney
2 tomatoes, peel, quarter

} add these 6 ingred.
simmer 10 min.

serves: 4-6

BEEF BRUSSELS

1 lb. round steak, cut ¼" thick slices
2 T. soy sauce
— marinade in soy sauce several hrs.

2 onions, sliced
2 T. veg. oil
— add meat to onions & oil / brown meat

2 T. flour
— sprinkle flour over top   stir in very well

1 c. sliced celery
10 brussels sprouts, quartered
— stir in these 2 vegetables / cook 3 min.

1 can water chestnuts, sliced
1 can mushrooms and liquid
1 T. soy sauce
1 T. brown sauce if available
1 c. water
5 beef bouillon cubes
— add these 6 ingred. / cook 4 min.

cooked rice
— serve with rice   serves: 4-6

1½ lb. round steak
½ t. salt
grinding pepper

} season and lay steak in shallow baking pan
bake 400° for 15 min.

16 oz. tomato sauce
2 T. lemon juice
1 bay leaf
3 to 4 cloves

} combine these 4 ingred. in pan
simmer 10 min.

1 onion, sliced
½ green pepper, sliced
4 oz. can mushrooms

} layer these 3 ingred. over steak
top with sauce   cover with foil
slit few holes for steam to escape
bake 325° for 1½ hr.

rice

} serve with rice

serves: 4

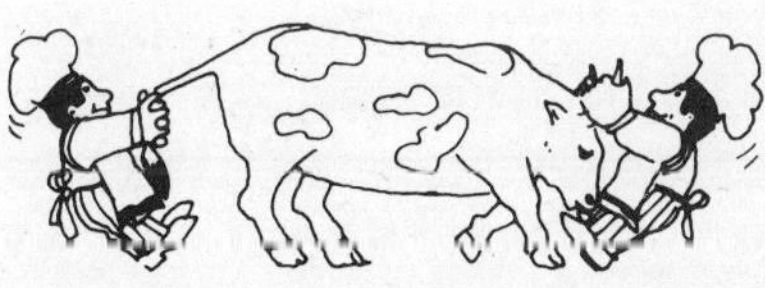

CINDERELLA STEW

1 whole med. pumpkin } cut off top of pumpkin to make lid
clean out seeds and fibers

butter
sugar } brush insides with butter
sprinkle lightly with sugar
replace lid
bake 350° for 45 min.
until inside is tender and shell is firm

2 lb. lean beef or pork, cubed
½ c. cornstarch
1 t. salt } combine these 3 ingred. in bag
toss to coat

2 T. veg. oil } brown meat in oil   reserve meat

2 onions, chopped
1 green pepper, chopped
1 T. veg. oil } saute veg. in pan 5 min.

(continued next page)

3 sweet potatoes, cubed
3 white potatoes, cubed
4 c. beef broth
1 c. water
1 can stewed tomatoes with liquid
½ t. oregano
1 bay leaf
1 t. salt
grinding pepper

add these 9 ingred. along with meat
simmer 20 min.

1 can small onions, drained
4 peaches, quartered
parsley

add onions and peaches   simmer 5 min.
set pumpkin on platter   fill pumpkin with stew
garnish with parsley

to serve scoop out part of pumpkin meat with stew

serves: 6

 MARINARA BUE

1 lb. round steak } pound steak to tenderize
slice into narrow strips

2 onions, sliced
1 stalk celery, sliced } combine these 3 ingred. with meat
1 T. veg. oil   brown meat

1 green pepper, sliced
1 c. brown rice } add these 4 ingred.
¼ t. garlic salt   cook stirring 6 min.
½ t. salt

1½ c. marinara spaghetti sauce } add these 2 ingred.
1½ c. water   cover
simmer 1½ hr.

serves: 4

1½ lb. sirloin steak, cubed
18 med. mushrooms, cleaned
18 water chestnuts
¾ c. burgundy
¾ c. veg. oil
2 T. worcestershire sauce
5 T. chili sauce
2 T. lemon juice
1 t. marjoram

combine these 9 ingred.
marinate several hrs.
alternate on skewers
broil in oven or barbeque
basting with marinade

serves: 6

SUKIYAKI

1 lb. sirloin, sliced paper thin
2 T. veg. oil

} brown meat

2/3 c. beef bouillon
1/3 c. soy sauce
2 T. sake or sherry
1 T. sugar
½ t. M.S.G.
½ t. salt
grinding pepper

} add these 7 ingred.
simmer 5 min.

1 bunch green onions, chopped
½ bunch spinach, chopped
1 can sliced bamboo shoots, drained
½ lb. sliced mushrooms

} add these 4 ingred.
cook 4 min.

cooked rice

} serve with rice

serves: 4

1 onion minced
2 strips bacon, diced

} fry onion and bacon 7 min.

¼ c. veg. oil
1/3 c. lemon juice
1 T. catsup
1 T. worcestershire sauce
1½ T. prepared horseradish
½ t. salt
grinding pepper

} add these 7 ingred. to make marinade

4 lg. cube steaks

} marinade steaks several hrs.
barbecue or broil
basting often

serves: 4

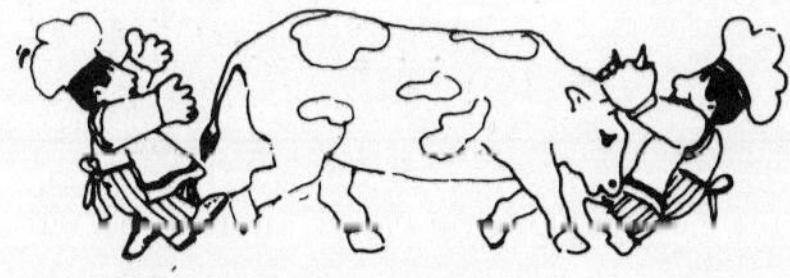

   DRESSED FLANK STEAK

1½ lb. flank steak, trimmed
1½ t. salt
½ t. paprika

> sprinkle seasonings over meat
> pound to tenderize

1 lg. onion, sliced
1 T. veg. oil

> saute onions 6 min.

1 c. bread crumbs
1 egg
¼ c. chopped celery
2 T. parsley
½ t. salt

> add these 5 ingred.
> toss lightly
> layer stuffing on meat
> roll up loosely
> tie to hold together

1 T. veg. oil

> brown meat on all sides

½ c. water
1 c. tomato juice or sauce
½ t. salt

> add these 3 ingred.
> cover
> simmer 1½ hr.

serves: 6

1 lb. ground beef
½ c. Italian seasoned bread crumbs
1/3 c. Parmesan cheese
1 T. instant minced onion
½ t. salt

} combine these 5 ingred.
shape into balls

1 T. veg. oil

} brown on all sides in oil

spaghetti for 6

} cook spaghetti as pkg. directs
drain
transfer to baking dish
top with meatballs

3 c. marinara spaghetti sauce
½ c. Parmesan cheese

} top with sauce then cheese
bake 350° for 25 min.

 ROLLS SWEET-SOUR

2½ lb. ground beef
½ c. minute rice
2 eggs
¼ t. garlic
grinding pepper

} combine these 5 ingred.

½ lb. brown sugar
juice of 3 lemons
1 c. tomato sauce
3 onions, chopped

} combine these 4 ingred.
add 1/3 of mixture to meat

1 very lg. head cabbage

} immerse cabbage in boiling water til leaves are pliable
remove 30 whole leaves
place 1 T. meat mixture in each leaf
roll up folding in sides of leaf to hold in filling
place open side down in baking dish
top with remaining sauce   cover with foil
bake 325° for 2 hrs.

tomato juice

} add juice if more moisture needed

makes 30 rolls

1 small cabbage, shredded
1 T. veg. oil
2 onions, chopped
1 clove garlic, smashed
1 green pepper, chopped
1 c. chopped celery
1 lb. ground beef
1 t. salt
grinding pepper

} combine these 9 ingred.
saute til meat looses redness

1 c. minute rice
1 can corn with liquid
½ t. seasoned salt

} mix in these 3 ingred.
beginning and ending with meat
layer in casserole with cabbage

1 can tomato soup
1 can tomato sauce

} pour soup and sauce over top
cover   bake 350° for 1 hr.   serves: 6

CABBAGE ROULADES

1 very lg. head cabbage

} par boil cabbage until leaves are pliable
reserve 20 whole leaves
coarsely chop remaining head

1 lb. ground beef
1 onion, minced
2 cloves garlic, minced
½ c. raw rice
1 egg
2 t. salt
grinding pepper

} combine these 7 ingred.
put 1 T. mixture on each leaf
roll up   fold sides toward center to hold in filling
layer ½ chopped cabbage in kettle
top with rolls seam sides down
top with remaining chopped cabbage

1 lb. sauerkraut, drained
1 28 oz. can tomatoes
1 t. Fines Herbes
1½ c. water
½ t. salt
grinding pepper

} top with these 6 ingred.
cover
simmer 50 min.

serves: 6

1 c. long grain or brown rice } cook rice as pkg. directs

1 lb. ground beef
1 onion, chopped
¼ green pepper, chopped
½ t. seasoned salt
½ t. salt
grinding pepper

} combine these 6 ingred.
saute until meat looses red color

1 sm. can mushrooms, drained
1 lb. can zucchini in tomato sauce

} add these 2 ingred.
combine all ingred. in casserole
bake 350° for 35 min.

serves: 4

  RYAN ROULETTE

1 lb. ground beef
1 egg
1 T. instant minced onion
¾ t. seasoned salt
½ t. salt

} combine these 5 ingred.

2 slices bread
¼ c. milk

} soak bread in milk
mash very well
mix into meat
roll meat out 8x12" on sheet of foil

1 lg. can sauerkraut

} wring juice from sauerkraut
chop fine
layer over meat

1 T. caraway seeds
¾ c. catsup

} spread these 2 ingred. over top
roll up jelly roll fashion
transfer to loaf pan remaining in foil
to omit pan washing
bake 350° for 1 hr.   serves: 6

BAKE A LA OKRA

1 pkg. frozen okra, thawed } layer ½ okra in bottom of casserole

1 lb. ground beef
1 onion, chopped
1 clove garlic, smashed
1 t. salt
grinding pepper

} saute these 5 ingred. til meat looses red color
layer in casserole
top with okra

½ c. tomato sauce } top with sauce
bake 350° for 35 min.
add more sauce if needed

serves: 4

NEAPOLITAN LASAGNA

1 lb. ground meat
1 onion, minced
1 T. veg. oil
1 clove garlic, smashed
1½ t. salt
grinding pepper

saute these 6 ingred.
until meat looses red color

1 #2 can tomatoes
1 c. tomato sauce
¼ t. oregano
3 T. chopped parsley

add these 4 ingred.
cover
simmer 40 min.
arrange 1/3 meat sauce in 12x8" baking dish

½ lb. lasagna noodles, cooked
¾ lb. sliced mozzarella cheese

layer with noodles
top with 1/3 mozzarella

1 lb. ricotta cheese
½ c. Parmesan cheese
¼ t. basil
1 egg

combine these 4 ingred.
top with ½ mixture
repeat layers ending with mozzarella

¼ c. Parmesan cheese

top with Parmesan   bake 350° for 40 min.   serves: 8

1 lg. onion, chopped
½ c. sliced mushrooms (opt.)
½ lb. ground beef   } saute these 5 ingred. til meat is light pink in color
1 T. margarine
½ t. salt

1 sm. head cabbage, shredded   } arrange layer of cabbage in casserole

½ T. caraway seeds   } sprinkle ½ of seeds over top
1 t. cumin seeds   } layer with ½ of meat   repeat layers

1 can tomato soup   } pour soup over top   cover   bake 350° for 1 hr.

¼ c. crushed cornflakes   } sprinkle flakes over top
                             bake 8 min. longer

serves: 4

    PARTY PIE

1 lb. ground beef
1 lg. onion, grated
¼ c. fine dry bread crumbs
1 egg
1½ t. seasoned salt
grinding pepper

} combine these 6 ingred.
pat in bottom and sides of casserole
bake 350° for 20 min.

3 lg. potatoes, cooked, drained
½ c. cottage cheese
¼ c. sour cream (opt.)
¼ c. milk
1 t. seasoned salt
¼ t. salt

} combine these 6 ingred.
beat til smooth
fill meat crust

½ can cond. cheddar cheese soup
½ t. mustard pd.

} combine these 2 ingred.
spread over casserole

paprika

} sprinkle with paprika
bake 350° for ½ hr.
until cheese is bubbly

serves: 4-6

1 lb. ground beef
1 onion, chopped
½ c. minute rice
1 egg
5 drop tabasco sauce
1 t. salt

} combine these 6 ingred.

4 green peppers

} core and seed peppers   stuff with meat

2 c. tomato sauce

} top with sauce   cover
bake 350° for 1½ hr.

Parmesan cheese

} top with Parmesan cheese
bake 5 min.

serves: 4

ROLL-UP THE GREAT

3 slices bread
½ c. water
} mash bread & water to paste

1½ lb. ground beef
1 egg
1 clove garlic, smashed
2 T. minced parsley
1 t. salt
grinding pepper
} add these 6 ingred.
mix well
on wax paper
roll into triangle   15" long, ½" thick

6 to 8 slices prosciutto or sliced ham
3 T. minced onion
3 T. raisins
3 T. pine nuts
3 T. parmesan
} layer these 5 ingred. over meat
beginning at narrow end
roll up jelly roll fashion
seal edges with a little water
wrap in wax paper

chill several hrs.

(continued next page)

3 T. veg. oil   }   brown meat on all sides in lg. pan

1 oz. tomato paste
1 c. water   add these 7 ingred. to pan
2 c. bouillon   cover
2 c. dry red wine   simmer 1 hr.
½ t. basil   add liquid if needed
½ t. salt   serve with pan sauces
grinding pepper

serves: 4-6

128   TAMALE PIE

1 c. cornmeal
1 c. cold water

} combine these 2 ingred. in pan

2 c. boiling water
1 t. salt
2 T. margarine

} grad. stir in these 3 ingred.
cook stirring constantly til thickened
cover   cook 5 min. to make mush   cool slightly

1 lb. ground beef
1 onion, chopped
1 green pepper, chopped
1½ t. chili pd.
1 t. seasoned salt
½ t. salt
grinding pepper

} saute these 7 ingred. til meat
looses red color

1 c. kidney beans, drained
1 can cond. tomato soup

} add these 2 ingred.
line greased baking dish with mush
top with meat   top with remaining mush

bake 375° for ½ hr.   serves: 6-8

2½ lb. ground beef
2 T. instant minced onion
1 egg
1½ t. salt
grinding pepper

} combine these 5 ingred.
shape into balls
brown on all sides

1 c. chopped celery
2 t. curry pd.
2 T. chopped parsley
2 c. water
4 beef bouillon cubes

} add these 5 ingred.
simmer 10 min.

3 T. cornstarch
¼ c. water

} combine these 2 ingred.
stir into meat cook til thickened

rice

} serve over rice

serves: 6-8

130 BEEF CASINO

¾ c. rice
3 T. chopped parsley

} cook rice as pkg. directs
mix in parsley

2 c. fresh bread crumbs
2 eggs, beaten
¼ c. milk

} combine these 3 ingred.
reserve

1/3 c. minced celery
1 onion, grated
1 clove garlic, smashed
1 t. salt
1 T. veg. oil

} saute these 5 ingred. 5 min.

2 lb. ground beef
¼ t. basil
½ t. salt
grinding pepper

} mix in these 4 ingred. along with bread mixture
pat on 11" square wax paper
spread rice over   roll up jelly roll fashion
place in 12x8" baking dish   seam side down

4 bacon slices

} arrange bacon over top
bake 350° for 1 hr. 20 min.

serves: 6

MOUSSAKA SKILLET

1½ lb. ground beef
1 lg. onion, chopped
1 t. salt

} saute these 3 ingred. 10 min.

2 unpeeled zucchini, sliced
1 eggplant, cubed
2 c. tomato sauce
1 t. oregano
1 t. basil
1 t. sugar
salt to taste

} add these 7 ingred.
simmer ½ hr.

¼ c. chopped parsley

} garnish with parsley

serves: 6

MERRY-GO ROUND

1 lb. ground beef
1 onion, minced
½ t. seasoned salt
1 t. salt
grinding pepper

saute these 5 ingred. til meat remains light pink
drain off any fat

¼ c. pickle relish
¼ t. mustard pd.
2 T. flour
1/3 c. water

stir in these 4 ingred.
cook til thickened
cool while making dough

2 c. biscuit mix
1¼ t. caraway seed
½ t. sage
¼ t. nutmeg
2/3 c. milk

combine these 5 ingred.
roll 12x9" rectangle   spread meat to ½" of sides
roll up jelly roll fashion   moisten edges with water
pinch shut   lay on greased shallow pan
bake 425° for 30 to 35 min.   slice to serve

1 pkg. gravy mix

prepare gravy as pkg. directs   serve with meat

serves: 4-6

HASH MASH

1 lb. ground beef
¾ c. mashed potatoes
1 onion, grated
1 egg
¼ c. catsup
1 t. worcestershire sauce
2 t. salt
grinding pepper

combine these 8 ingred.
shape into 6 patties
fry until browned on both sides

6 slices cheddar cheese

top with cheese
cover 1 min. to soften cheese

serves: 6

CHILI CON CARNE DELUXE

3 c. dried pinto beans } cook beans as pkg. directs

3 lb. ground beef
4 onions, chopped
6 clove garlic, smashed
¼ c. chili pd.
¼ c. paprika
1 t. ground cloves

} saute these 6 ingred. 10 min.

2 T. cumin seeds
1 bay leaf
1 T. coriander seeds
1½ T. oregano
1 t. basil

} combine these 5 ingred. in a pie pan
toast in 350° oven 10 min. stirring often
pound or blend to a powder
add to meat

3 c. tomato sauce
1 lg. can tomatoes and juice
5 c. water
10 beef bouillon cubes

} add these 4 ingred.
cover
simmer gently 1 day
stir in cooked beans

serves: 12

1 lb. ground beef
1 clove garlic, smashed
2 onions, chopped
1 t. salt

saute these 4 ingred. 10 min.

½ t. oregano
½ t. crushed red peppers (opt.)
½ green pepper, chopped
1 lg. can kidney beans, drained
2 c. tomato sauce
2 t. chili pd.

add these 6 ingred.
cover
simmer 1 hr.

serves: 4

MEAT LOAF PARMENTIER

1 lb. ground beef
½ c. oatmeal
1 onion, chopped
1 egg
1 t. worchestershire sauce
¼ t. marjoram
¼ t. garlic salt
2 t. salt
grinding pepper
} combine these 9 ingred.
pack ½ in meat loaf pan

3 boiled eggs, shelled
1 can mushroom slices, drained
} arrange these 2 ingred.
in center of loaf
top with remaining meat
bake 350° for 1 hr.

2 c. mashed potatoes, seasoned
} frost with potatoes

1 T. margarine
2 T. Parmesan cheese
} top with these 2 ingred.
bake 15 min. longer

serves: 4

1 lb. ground beef
1 onion, chopped
2 carrots, sliced thin
2 stalks celery, sliced
3 crocked neck yellow squash, sliced
¼ t. garlic salt
1 t. salt

} saute these 7 ingred. 15 min.

1 can cond. cream of mushroom soup } stir in soup
transfer to casserole

1 tomato, sliced
1 c. potato chip crumbs

} top with tomato and crumbs
bake 350° for 35 min.

serves: 4

ENCHILADAS

1 c. tomato sauce
1 clove garlic, smashed
1 sm. onion, grated
1½ t. cumin
1 T. instant green pepper
taco sauce to taste
salt to taste
grinding pepper

} combine these 8 ingred.
simmer 1 hr.

½ lb. ground beef
1 onion, chopped
½ t. salt

} saute these 3 ingred. 8 min.

8 tortillas

} dip tortillas in sauce
fill with meat   roll up
layer seam side down in baking pan   top with sauce
bake 350° for 15 min.

¼ c. chopped ripe olives
½ c. grated cheese

} top with these 2 ingred.
bake 10 min.

serves 4

2 c. boiling water
1/3 c. wild rice
1/3 c. brown rice

} combine these 3 ingred.
let stand 15 min.
drain

1 c. chicken broth
3 oz. can mushroom pieces undrained
1 t. celery salt
1 t. onion salt
¼ t. garlic salt
½ t. paprika
¼ t. liquid smoke (opt.)

} add these 7 ingred. to rice

½ lb. ground beef
1 onion, chopped
½ t. salt

} saute these 3 ingred. 10 min.
combine in casserole with rice mixture
cover
bake 325° for 1½ hrs.

serves: 4

 BATATA-CHALATA

1 lb. ground beef
1 onion, chopped
1 clove garlic, smashed
2 t. chili pd.
1½ t. salt

} saute these 5 ingred. 10 min.

2 c. tomato sauce
¼ c. catsup
½ c. water
1 T. lemon juice
¾ c. corn, drained
½ c. chopped ripe olives

} add these 6 ingred.

2 c. mashed potatoes

} line 9x9" cake pan with potatoes
fill with meat mixture
bake 350° for ½ hr.

1 c. grated cheddar cheese

} sprinkle cheese over
bake 15 min.

serves: 6

1½ lbs. ground beef
1 onion, chopped
2 c. diced celery
¾ t. salt

saute these 4 ingred. 10 min.
layer ½ in casserole

1 pkg. peas, thawed
1 can cond. cream of mushroom soup
2 T. milk
¼ t. salt
grinding pepper

combine these 5 ingred.
pour 1/3 over meat
repeat layers

1 c. cornflakes, crumbs

top with crumbs
bake 375° for ½ hr.

serves: 6

PICADILLO

1 lb. ground beef
2 onions, grated
2 cloves garlic, smashed
1½ t. salt
grinding pepper

} saute these 5 ingred. 10 min.

3 tomatoes, peeled, chopped
2 apples, chopped
2 canned jalapeno chilies, chopped
½ c. raisins
8 stuffed olives, sliced
¼ t. allspice

} add these 6 ingred.
uncovered
simmer 5 min.

½ c. pine nuts (if available) } stir in nuts

cooked rice or pinto beans } serve with rice or / and beans

serves: 4-6

SAFFRON SIMMER

1 lb. ground beef
1 clove garlic, smashed
1 T. margarine } saute these 5 ingred. 8 min.
1 t. salt
grinding pepper

2 tomatoes, peeled, quartered
2 onions, cut in rings
1 stalk celery, minced
4 oz. can mushrooms & liquid
¼ t. saffron } add these 9 ingred.
1 c. minute rice   cover
1 can corn, drained   simmer 10 min.
½ green pepper, chopped
10½ oz. can beef consomme

serves: 6

BEEF A LA MODE

1½ lb. ground beef
1 onion, chopped
1 clove garlic, smashed
½ green pepper, chopped
1 stalk celery, chopped
1½ T. chili pd.
1½ T. salt
grinding pepper

} saute these 8 ingred. 10 min.

1 c. tomato sauce

} stir in sauce   simmer 15 min.
transfer to 9" sq. baking dish

1 c. flour
¾ c. yellow cornmeal
2 t. baking pd.
½ t. baking soda
½ t. salt

} combine these 5 ingred.

½ c. buttermilk
2 eggs
1 T. honey

} mix in these 3 ingred.   stir only to moisten
spoon over meat
bake 400° for ½ hr.   serves: 4

CASSOLITA

1 lb. ground beef
1 onion, chopped
1 clove garlic, smashed   } saute these 6 ingred. 10 min.
1 T. chili pd.
1½ t. salt
grinding pepper

½ c. sliced black olives
1 c. tomato sauce   } add these 3 ingred.
1/3 c. water

6 tortillas
6 slices cheddar cheese   } cover bottom of casserole with meat sauce
top with tortilla   meat sauce   cheese
repeat layers ending with cheese
bake 350° for 35 to 40 min.

serves: 4

 PIEBURGER

1 lb. ground beef
1 onion, chopped
½ c. chopped celery   saute these 7 ingred. 10 min.
¾ t. chili pd.
1 t. seasoned salt
1 t. salt
grinding pepper

¼ c. flour   grad. stir in flour

6 oz. can tomato paste   add these 3 ingred.
¼ c. water   uncovered
1 t. worcestershire sauce   cook until thickened

1½ c. flour   combine these 4 ingred.
½ t. salt   cut together with a fork
½ c. Kraft canned grated Amer. cheese   until mixed and crumbly
½ c. veg. oil

4-5 T. water   add water to make stiff dough roll out to fit 9" pie pan
                              fill with meat mixture   bake 400° for 35 min.

1 lb. ground beef
1 onion, chopped
¼ t. salt

} saute these 3 ingred. 8 min.

1 pkg. taco seasoning mix
2 c. tomato sauce
2 c. cooked macaroni

} stir in these 3 ingred.
transfer to casserole
cover

bake 325° for ½ hr.

serves: 4

CHILI-O CASSER-O

1½ lb. ground beef
1 onion, chopped
1 clove garlic, smashed
¼ t. celery salt
1 t. salt

} saute these 5 ingred. 10 min.

2 c. tomato sauce
1 lb. can kidney beans, drained
2½ t. chili pd.

} add these 3 ingred.
simmer 8 min.
transfer to casserole

½ c. flour
½ c. cornmeal
1 T. baking pd.
1 T. honey
½ t. salt
2 T. veg. oil
1 egg

} combine these 7 ingred.
mix with fork to moisten only
spread over casserole
bake 350° for 30 to 35 min.

serves: 6

POTATOES DUBLIN

2 T. vinegar
1 t. celery salt
1 t. mustard pd.
2 t. sugar
½ t. salt
3 lg. potatoes, cooked, cubed

} combine these 6 ingred.
chill well

2 c. grated cabbage
1 12 oz. can corned beef, cubed
¼ c. minced dill pickles
¼ c. chopped green onion

} add these 4 ingred.

1 c. mayonnaise
¼ c. milk
½ t. salt

} combine these 3 ingred.
lightly toss in

serves: 6-8

TONGUE HOT OR COLD

4 to 5 lb. tongue

} soak tongue in water in refrig. over night
drain

3 bay leaves
1 clove garlic
1 t. whole peppercorns
½ t. cloves
1 onion, sliced
1 T. horseradish
2½ t. salt
water to cover

} add these 8 ingred. to tongue
cover
gently simmer 3½ hr.
pour off water
cut skin off root end
slice diagonally to serve

serves: 6-8

6 slices calf liver
¼ c. flour
¼ t. thyme
½ t. mustard pd.
1½ t. salt
grinding pepper

combine these 6 ingred. in bag
shake well to coat

2 T. margarine
1 bunch green onions, chopped
½ t. instant minced garlic

combine these 3 ingred. with liver in pan
quickly saute til browned on both sides

1 orange, thinly sliced

add orange
cook ½ min.

serves: 4-6

LIVER EAST INDIAN

¼ t. cayenne pepper
½ t. ginger
1 t. tumeric
¼ t. garlic salt
½ t. salt
grinding pepper
1 T. red wine vinegar

} combine these 7 ingred.

1 lb. calf liver

} coat liver with spices

1 T. veg. oil
1 onion, chopped

} saute liver with these 2 ingred.
2 min. on each side

1 t. lemon juice

} sprinkle juice over top

rice

} serve with rice

serves: 4

ORIENTAL INFLUENCE

1 lb. calf liver, cut strips
2 T. soy sauce
½ t. sugar
1 T. water
1 T. cornstarch

combine these 5 ingred.
marinate 25 min.
drain

3 T. veg. oil
1 green pepper, cut in strips
1 bunch green onions, chopped
1 t. salt
grinding pepper

saute liver with these 5 ingred.
until browned on both sides

serves: 4

LIVER DELICACY

2 lg. onions, sliced
pinch sage
¼ c. margarine
1 T. olive oil

} saute these 4 ingred. 5 min.

1¾ lb. calf liver
¼ c. flour
1 t. salt
grinding pepper

} combine these 4 ingred. in bag
toss to coat
add to onions
quickly cook 3 min. on both sides
transfer to serving dish

1 T. beef broth
1 T. minced parsley

} add these 2 ingred. to pan
scrape sides and bottom
pour over liver

serves: 6

BROCHETTE DE LIVER

1½ lb. liver, cut 1½" sq.
6 strips bacon, cut in 3rds.
12 cherry tomatoes
12 water chestnuts
12 small canned onions, drained

} arrange these 5 ingred.
on 12 skewers
place in baking dish

¾ c. veg. oil
¼ c. lemon juice
1 clove garlic, smashed
1 t. instant minced onion
1 t. parsley
1 t. tarragon
1 T. prepared mustard
1 T. worcestershire sauce

} combine these 8 ingred.
pour over skewers
refrig. 1 hr.
turning occassionally
remove from marinade
broil about 5 min. on each side basting with marinade
until bacon is done

serves: 6

PAKISTAN FESTIVAL

2 T. veg. oil
2 lg. onions, chopped

} gently saute onions 8 min.
reserve onions

¼ t. pd. cumin
1 T. tumeric
½ t. ginger
¼ t. garlic salt
⅛ t. cayenne pepper
1 t. salt
2 lb. lamb, ½" cubes

} combine these 7 ingred. in bag
toss to coat meat
brown meat in onion pan
return onions to pan

1 c. plain yogurt

} add yogurt
cover
simmer 45 min.
or until tender

¾ toasted almonds
cooked rice

} serve over rice
topped with almonds

serves: 6

MANDARIN CHOPS

4 thick lamb chops } brown chops on both sides

1 c. uncooked rice } place rice in casserole / top with meat

1 can mandarin oranges, drained
2½ c. beef bouillon
½ t. mint
½ t. seasoned salt
grinding pepper

} top meat with these 5 ingred.
cover
bake 350° about 1 hr.
add liquid if necessary

serves: 4

EGGPLANT ARABY

6 sm. eggplant

} cut off 1 end of each eggplant
scoop out pulp leaving shells in tact
chop pulp

1 lb. ground lamb
1 onion, grated
3 T. raw rice
1 T. catsup
1 T. minced mint
1 t. dill weed
½ t. cinnamon
1 t. salt
grinding pepper

} combine these 9 ingred.
with pulp
stuff shells
place in baking dish

¾ c. beef bouillon
¾ c. tomato juice

} add liquid
cover
bake 350° for 1 hr.

serve hot or cold

serves: 6

6 pork chops
salt
pepper

} season and brown chops on both sides
transfer to casserole

1 c. uncooked rice
1 lg. tomato, sliced
1 lg. onion, sliced
1 T. instant green pepper
1 t. salt
grinding pepper
4 c. beef bouillon

} top chops with these 7 ingred.
cover
bake 1 hr.

3 c. cubed winter squash
6 stalks celery, cut 1" pieces
1 lb. green beans

} pile vegetables around chops
cover
bake ½ hr.

serves: 6

PORK FIESTA

8 1" thick pork chops
¼ c. flour
pinch thyme
1 t. salt
grinding pepper

} combine these 5 ingred. in bag
shake to coat meat
brown on first side
turn

1 lg onion, chopped

} add onions
brown second side

1 pkg. beef flavored Au Jus mix
   or 1 pkg. onion soup mix
2 c. water

} add these 2 ingred.
cover
simmer 1 hr.

4 bananas, cut ½ lengthwise
1 green pepper, cut strips
4 oz. can chopped pimento

} top with these 3 ingred.

spaghetti or rice

} serve with your choice

serves: 8

SWEETY HAM CASSEROLE

6 slices cooked ham } layer ham in baking dish

1 c. medium white sauce
2 eggs, beaten
½ c. grated cheddar cheese
¼ t. salt
grinding pepper } combine these 5 ingred.

4 cooked sweet potatoes, sliced } fold in potatoes
pile on top of ham

¼ c. grated cheddar cheese } top with cheese
bake 350° for ½ hr.

serves: 6

CAULIFLOWER DANISH

1 lg. whole cauliflower

}

blanch in boiling salted water 12 min.
drain
transfer to round casserole

1 onion, diced
2 T. margarine

}

saute onion til soft

1 c. minced cooked Danish ham
2 pimiento stuffed olives, minced
1 T. chopped parsley
2 c. fresh bread crumbs
1 egg
1/3 c. milk
1 t. salt
grinding pepper

}

blend in these 8 ingred.
carefully stuff in between flowerettes
arrange any left over around base

2 T. margarine
¼ c. parmesan

}

top with these 2 ingred.
bake uncovered 350° for 20 min.

serves: 4-6

QUICK E OMELET

1 c. diced cooked ham
1 green pepper, diced
2 T. margarine

} saute these 3 ingred. 4 min.

4 eggs

} break eggs into mixture
stir to mix together
cook until semi-firm

4 slices cheese

} top with cheese
fold in half

serves: 2

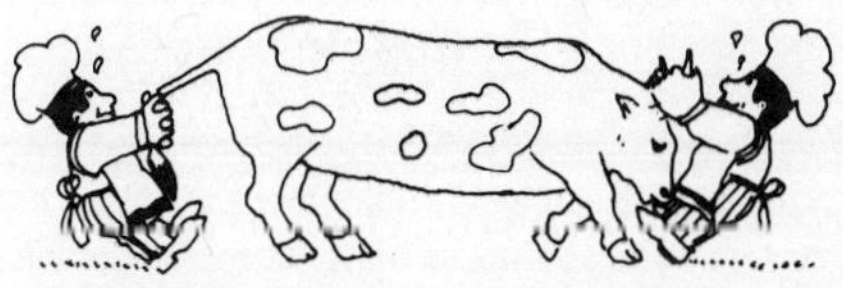

  SPICY EGG 'N HAM BAKE

3 T. margarine
3 T. flour
1 t. mustard pd.
¾ t. salt
grinding pepper

gently heat & blend together these 5 ingred.

1½ c. milk
1 t. prepared horseradish
1 T. worcestershire sauce
1 T. chili sauce
dash tabasco sauce

grad. blend in these 5 ingred.
cook until thickened

6 boiled eggs, sliced
2 c. diced cooked ham
½ c. sliced ripe olives
¾ c. diced cheddar cheese

layer these 4 ingred. along with sauce in casserole
ending with sauce
bake 350° for ½ hr.

serves: 4-5

CASSEROLE BELLE HELENE 165

¼ c. margarine
¼ c. flour

} blend these 2 ingred. over gentle heat

1½ c. chicken bouillon
½ c. milk
¼ t. mace
salt to taste
grinding pepper

} grad. blend in these 5 ingred.

3 boiled eggs, sliced
1 pkg. Danish ham, sliced
24 cooked asparagus spears

} layer these 3 ingred. along with sauce in casserole
ending with sauce
bake 350° for 20 min.

paprika

} sprinkle paprika over top

serves: 4-5

MAC STACK

12 slices bread
mayonnaise
mustard

} spread slices with mustard & mayonnaise

12 slices cooked ham
6 apples, sliced
12 slices cheddar cheese

} layer these 3 ingred. over each slice

sesame seeds

} sprinkle sesame over top
broil to melt cheese

serves: 6

4 slices toasted bread   }   heat soup
1 can cond. Bean with Bacon Soup   }   divide over toast

4 fried eggs   }   top with eggs

serves: 4

DAIRYLAND DREAM

1 lb. link pork sausage

} cook sausage as pkg. directs
drain off most fat

½ c. chopped green onion
½ green pepper, chopped

} saute onions & peppers in drippings 4 min.

1 c. sour cream
1 c. cottage cheese
1 c. tomato sauce
1½ T. flour
½ t. seasoned salt
grinding pepper

} blend in these 6 ingred.

6 oz. noodles

} cook and drain noodles
combine all in casserole

½ c. Parmesan cheese

} top with cheese
bake 350° for 25 min.

serves: 4-6

PRESTO PIZZA

2 c. biscuit mix
2/3 c. water

} blend water & mix
knead 10 times
roll out to fit pizza pan or baking dish

1½ c. canned spaghetti sauce
1 lg. onion, chopped
1 can sliced mushrooms
3 hot dogs, sliced

} top with these 4 ingred.

½ c. Parmesan cheese

} top with cheese
bake 370° for ½ hr.

serves: 4

FRANKLY BEANS

2 c. cooked potatoes, sliced
1 onion, chopped
2 T. bacon drippings

} brown potatoes & onions

2 c. cooked green beans, drained
6 hot dogs sliced
1 t. minced parsley
¼ c. veg. oil
¼ c. vinegar
¼ t. sugar
1½ t. salt
grinding pepper

} combine these 8 ingred.
with potatoes in casserole
uncovered
bake 375° for ½ hr.

serves: 6

SAUERKRAUT SUPPER

4 c. sauerkraut, partially drained
1 onion, diced
½ t. caraway seed
dash white pepper
1 lb. hot dogs, sliced

} combine these 5 ingred.

2 bay leaves

} lay bay leaves on bottom of casserole

2 c. seasoned mashed potatoes

} top with kraut mixture
make a border of potatoes around edges

½ c. grated cheddar cheese

} top with cheese
uncovered
bake 350° for 20 min.

serves: 6

 CURRY SCURRY

1½ T. margarine
1 onion, sliced

} saute onion 5 min.

1½ c. canned tomatoes
1 c. sliced mushrooms
¾ t. curry pd.
¼ t. salt
grinding pepper
4 boiled knockwurst, sliced

} add these 6 ingred.
bring to a boil
make 4 wells in mixture

4 eggs

} break 1 egg in each well
cover
cook 5 min. or until set

4 slices toast

} serve egg on toast
top with veg. & sauce

serves: 4

FLAP JACKS CONTINENTAL

2¼ c. flour
8 t. baking pd.
2 T. sugar
½ t. salt
1 egg
2 c. milk
¼ c. veg. oil
2 hot dogs, diced

combine these 8 ingred.
thin with water if necessary
drop by ¼ c. at a time on greased griddle
brown on both sides

serves: 4

FRANK PRANK

4 lg. green peppers } core & seed peppers
par boil in boiling salted water 5 min.
drain

4 hot dogs, diced } combine these 6 ingred.
1 c. drained corn — stuff peppers
1 can cond. cream of celery soup — put into casserole
1 t. curry pd. — add ¼ c. water to casserole
¼ t. salt — cover
grinding pepper — bake 350° for ½ hr.

serves: 4

SUPER SANDWITCH 175

2 slices bread
mustard
sliced salami
sliced cheddar cheese

} make sandwich with these ingred.

1 egg, beaten
1 T. milk
⅛ t. salt

} combine these 3 ingred.
dip both sides of sandwich in egg
taking care not to let it open

gently fry on greased griddle
brown on both sides til cheese is melted

serves: 1

CASSEROLE EPICURE

2 onions, sliced
1 T. veg. oil

} saute onions 5 min.

1 c. rice
½ t. salt

} add rice
stir fry 5 min.

2 c. beef bouillon
2 c. diced cooked beef

} add these 2 ingred.
cook 20 min.

saltine crackers
2 tomatoes, sliced

} layer crackers over bottom of casserole
layer tomatoes over top with beef-rice mixture

½ c. tomato sauce
2 tomatoes, sliced
¼ t. salt

} top with these 3 ingred.
cover
bake 350° for ½ hr.

¾ c. sour cream
¼ c. Major Grey chutney
¼ c. raisins

} combine these 3 ingred.
spread over top

¼ c. grape nut cereal

} sprinkle cereal over top
bake 5 min. uncovered

serves: 4-6

GRAND STRAWBERRY ICE CREAM

1 qt. vanilla ice cream, softened
1 c. heavy cream, whipped
1 t. vanilla
1/3 c. sugar
¼ c. Grand Marnier liqueur
2 T. Kirsch

combine these 6 ingred.
beat smooth
put in freezer

4 c. sliced strawberries

add berries 1 hr. before serving

whole strawberries
mint sprigs

garnish to serve

serves: 12

 PUMPKIN RICE PUDDING

½ med. orange, unpeeled
½ lemon, unpeeled
1½ c. water
1 carrot, pared, sliced
1½ lb. pumpkin, peeled, diced
2 c. sugar

combine these 6 ingred.
cook uncovered 40 min. or til liquid is almost absorbed & mixture sheets off spoon

⅛ t. ginger
⅛ t. cloves
1 t. cinnamon
3½ c. cooked rice

mix in these 4 ingred.
this may be kept several days in refrig.

whipped cream

serve with cream

serves: 8

RHUBARB MANIA

3 c. fresh or frozen rhubarb
½ c. water } gently cook rhubarb until tender

1½ c. applesauce
sugar to taste } stir in these 2 ingred.

sour cream or
whipped cream } serve hot or cold
topped with cream

serves: 4

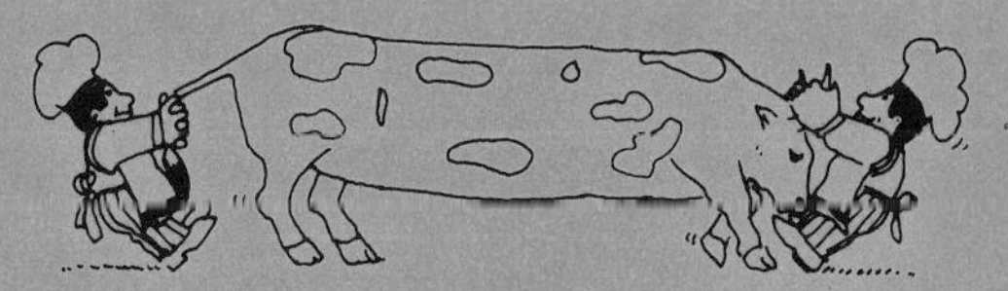

COFFEE CLOUD

½ c. cold water
2 pkg. plain gelatin

} sprinkle gelatin over water
let stand 5 min.

2 c. very strong coffee
½ c. sugar

} combine these 2 ingred.
bring to boil
add gelatin to dissolve

8 ice cubes

} stir in ice to dissolve
chill til slightly thickened

1 pkg. dream whip

} whip cream as pkg. directs
beat into gelatin

4 egg whites

} beat whites til stiff
fold into gelatin
divide into 6 dessert dishes
refrig. til firm

serves: 6

LIME YOGURT PIE

1 pkg. unflavored gelatin
6 oz. can limeade concentrate

} sprinkle gelatin over limeade
soften 5 min.
dissolve over boiling water

¼ c. sugar
½ c. plain yoghurt

} stir in these 2 ingred.
chill til partially set

1 pkg. Dream Whip topping mix

} beat cream as pkg. directs
fold into gelatin

9" prepared graham cracker crust

} fill pie shell

1 oz. chocolate

} grate chocolate over top
chill til firm

serves: 6

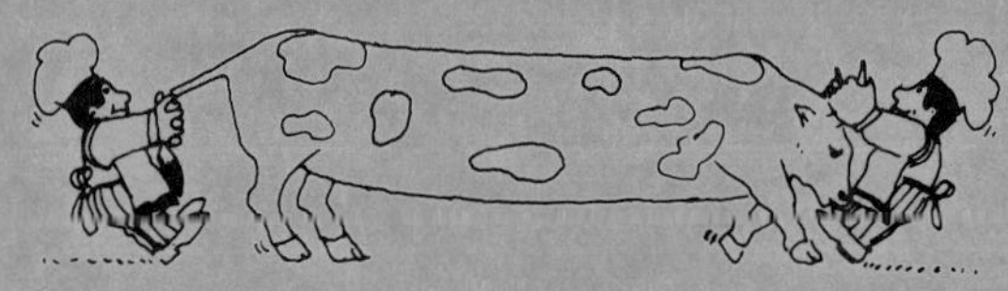

 FROZEN LUSCIOUS LEMON

3 egg yolks, beaten
½ c. sugar
1/3 c. lemon juice
grated rind of ½ lemon

> combine these 4 ingred.
> cook over boiling water
> stirring til thick
> cool

1 sm. box vanilla wafers, crumbled
½ c. ground almonds
¼ c. sugar
1 stick margarine

> combine these 4 ingred.
> pat on bottom & sides
> of 10" pie pan to make crust

1 c. cream

> beat cream stiff
> mix into lemon filling

3 egg whites
4 T. sugar

> beat whites til stiff
> grad. beat sugar in whites
> fold into lemon mixture
> fill pie shell
> freeze

let stand at room temp ½ hr. before serving

1½ c. pd. sugar
½ c. margarine
} beat these 2 ingred. til creamy

1 sm. can fruit cocktail, drained
1 sm. can sliced peaches, drained
} mix in fruit

1 pkg. dessert whip topping mix
} whip cream as pkg. directs
fold ½ into fruit

9" baked pie shell
} fill shell

top with remaining cream
chill at least 12 hrs.

serves: 8

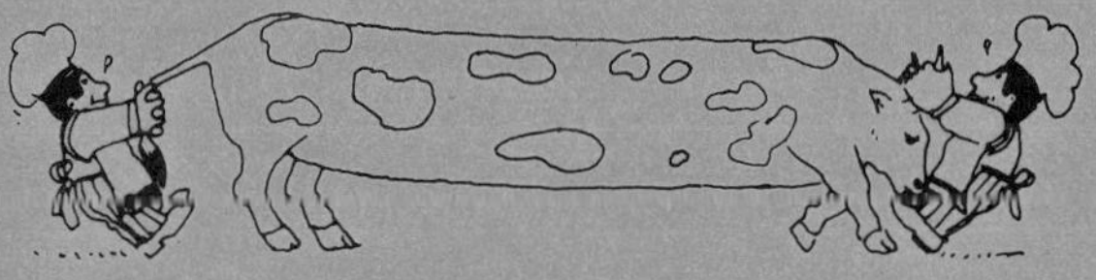

RUM CREME FREEZE

4 egg whites — beat whites til stiff

4 egg yolks
4 T. sugar —
beat yolks well
grad. beat in sugar til thick & pale in color
about 8 min.
fold in whites

1 pkg. Dream Whip topping mix or
  1 c. whipping cream — whip cream til stiff

2 T. rum —
mix in rum
fold into egg mixture

baked pie shell — fill pie shell

¼ c. toasted slivered almonds —
top with almonds
freeze 8 hrs.
let stand at room temp. 20 min. to mellow before
serving

serves: 8

OATMEAL NUT CRUST PEACH PIE

1 c. oatmeal

} spread oatmeal on baking sheet
toast in 350° oven 10 min.

¼ c. wheat germ
2/3 c. chopped walnuts
3 T. sugar
1/3 c. softened margarine

} mix in these 4 ingred.
press on bottom & sides of 9" pie plate
bake 350° for 10 min.

1 lg. can peaches & juice
1½ T. cornstarch mix with 2 T. juice

} combine these 2 ingred. in pan
cook stirring til thickened
pour into crust
bake 350° for 25 min.

¾ c. cottage cheese
¾ c. sour cream
2 T. sugar

} puree these 3 ingred.
top pie

serves: 6

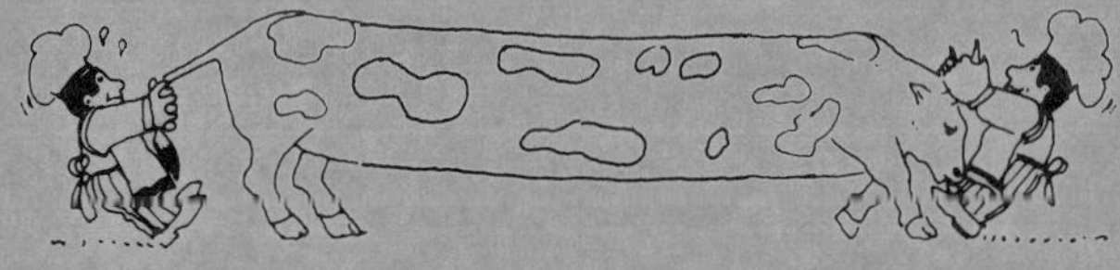

PLUM KUCHEN

2 T. margarine
1 egg plus milk to fill ½ c.   } combine these 3 ingred.
¼ c. honey

1¼ c. flour   } sift in these 3 ingred.
1 t. baking pd.   blend with fork
½ t. salt   pat dough into bottom & sides of 9" layer cake pan

8 lg. plums, peeled, sliced
¼ c. chopped pecans   } combine these 4 ingred.
½ c. brown sugar   layer over dough
1 T. flour

1 egg
¼ c. sugar   } combine these 3 ingred.
2 T. cream   layer over plums

                                      } lightly sprinkle top with nutmeg
nutmeg   bake 350° for 15 min.
                                        325° for 25 min.   serves: 6

1 pkg. yellow cake mix
1 c. water
2 eggs
¼ c. veg. oil

} combine these 4 ingred.
beat 2 min.

1/3 c. sesame seeds
1 c. grated carrots

} fold in these 2 ingred.
pour into greased & floured 13x9x2" cake pan
bake 350° for 30 min.

pd. sugar

} sift pd. sugar over top

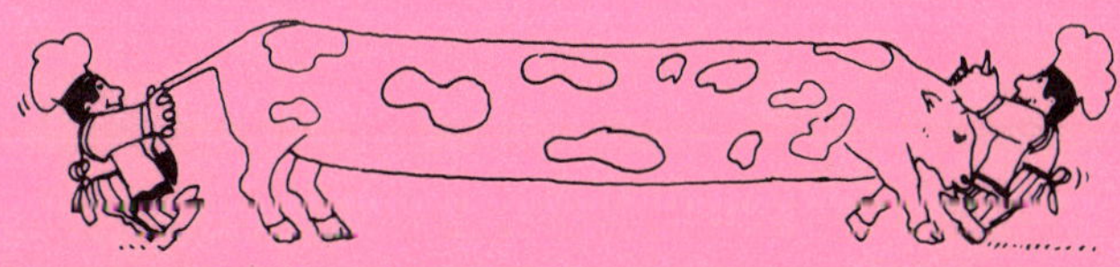

PUFF PASTE COFFEE CAKE

1 c. flour
¼ t. salt
½ c. margarine

combine these 3 ingred.
cut together with fork

2 T. cold water

mix in water to form dough
pat into bottom & ½ way up sides of 9x9" pan

¼ c. ground almonds
2 T. sugar

sprinkle these 2 ingred. over crust

1 c. water
½ c. margarine

combine these 2 ingred. in pan
bring to boil

1 c. flour

add flour all at once
stir til dough leaves sides & forms ball
remove from heat

3 eggs

1 at a time beat in eggs

(continued next page)

1 t. almond extract   } stir in extract
fill pastry shell
bake 425° for 35 min.

½ c. pd. sugar
1 T. hot water
¼ t. almond extract   } mix these 3 ingred. til smooth
drizzle over cake while hot

almond halves   } decorate with almonds
serve warm or cold

serves: 6

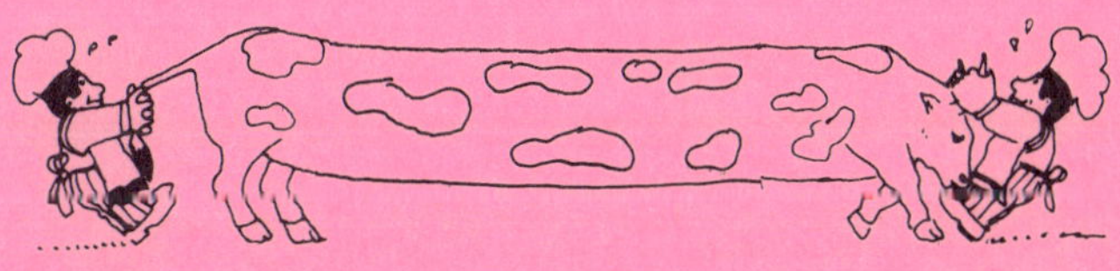

CECI CHIFFON

15½ oz. can garbanzo beans, drained
1/3 c. milk
3 egg yolks
¼ c. honey
½ t. cinnamon
¾ t. vanilla

combine & puree these 6 ingred.

3 egg whites

beat whites til stiff
fold in
pour into greased casserole

nutmeg
cinnamon
sugar

sprinkle top with these 3 ingred.
bake 350° for 45 min.

serves: 4

BLUEBERRY FLAT CAKES

1 pkg. corn muffin mix

} prepare muffins as pkg. directs
drop by 2 T. per cake on
greased cooky sheet 2" apart

1 c. blueberries
1/3 c. sour cream
2 T. honey

} combine these 3 ingred.
mound 1 T. berries on top of each cake
bake as directed on muffin pkg.

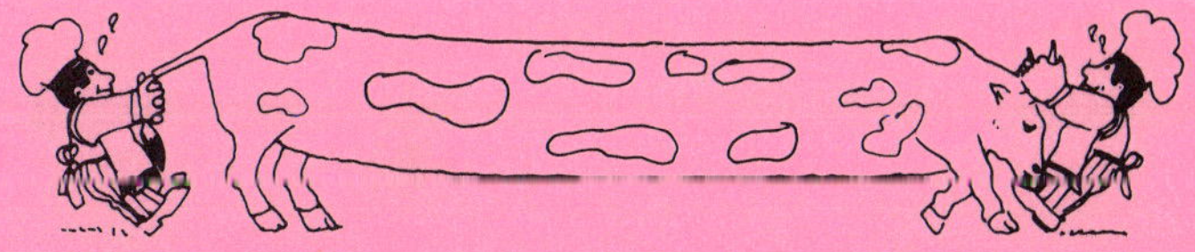

COOKY CRUNCHES

1 c. sesame seeds
} place seeds on cooky sheet
bake 350° for 8 min. or light brown
stirring occassionally

½ c. veg. oil
1 egg
½ c. brown sugar
¼ c. honey
} combine these 4 ingred.
beat til creamy

1 c. flour
1 t. baking pd.
¾ t. baking soda
½ t. salt
} beat in these 4 ingred.

1 t. vanilla
½ c. coconut
½ c. hulled sunflower seeds
1 c. oatmeal
} mix in these 4 ingred.
drop by t. on ungreased sheets
bake 350° for 13-15 min.

36 cookies

A reference guide to the calorie, protein, carbohydrate and fat content of many common foods and frequently used ingredients. This information should take much of the guesswork out of planning nutritious meals. It is important for dieters to note that calories do count. Fats and oils contribute over twice as many calories (9 calories per gram), alcohol or ethanol furnishes nearly 75% more calories (7 calories per gram) than do carbohydrates and proteins at 4 calories per gram. A more comprehensive listing of food values can be found in the inexpensive U.S. Department of Agriculture House and Garden Bulletin No. 72, "Nutritive Value of Foods."   Do not confuse the weight in grams for calories. Multiply protein and carbohydrate grams by 4 and the grams of fat by 9 to get the approx. number of calories.

	PORTION	CALORIES	PROTEIN (grams)	CARBOHY-DRATES (grams)	FAT (grams)
Almonds, shelled, whole	½ cup	425	13	14	38
Apple juice, canned or bottled	8 ounces	120	trace	30	trace
Apple pie, 2 crust, 9-inch	1/8	300	3	51	15
Apples, raw, 3-inch diameter	One	70	trace	18	trace
Applesauce, canned, sweetened	1 cup	230	1	61	trace
Applesauce, canned, unsweetened	1 cup	100	1	26	trace
Apricots, fresh	3 medium	55	1	14	trace
Apricots, dried	10 halves	100	2	25	trace
Apricots, canned with syrup	1 cup	220	2	57	trace
Artichoke, French	One	50			trace
Artichoke hearts, canned	Four	20			trace
Asparagus spears, cooked	4 medium	10	1	2	trace
Asparagus soup, cream of	1 cup	215	7	16	14
Avocado	½ medium	185	3	7	19

	PORTION	CALORIES	PROTEIN	CARBOHY.	FAT
Bacon, broiled or fried	2 strips	90	5	1	8
Bananas	1 medium	100	1	26	trace
Beans, green, cooked, cut	1 cup	30	2	7	trace
Beans, kidney, canned	1 cup	230	15	42	1
Beans, Lima, cooked	1 cup	260	16	49	1
Beef, hamburger, lean	3 ounces	185	23	0	10
Beef, hamburger, regular	3 ounces	245	21	0	17
Beef, pot roast	3 ounces	245	21	0	17
Beef, rib roast	3 ounces	375	17	0	34
Beef, round steak, lean	3 ounces	160	26	0	5
Beef, sirloin steak	3 ounces	330	20	0	27
Beer, lager	12 ounces	150	1	14	0
Beets, cooked, sliced	1 cup	55	2	12	trace
Blackberries, fresh	1 cup	85	2	19	1
Black-eyed peas, cooked	1 cup	190	13	34	1
Blueberries, fresh	1 cup	85	1	21	1
Bouillon, beef or chicken	1 cube	5	1	trace	trace
Bran flakes (40% bran)	1 cup	105	4	28	1
Bread, white	1 slice	60	2	12	1
Bread, whole-wheat	1 slice	55	2	11	1
Breadcrumbs, dry, grated	1 cup	390	13	73	5
Broccoli, cooked	1 cup	45	6	8	1
Brussels sprouts, cooked	1 cup	55	7	10	1
Butter	½ cup	810	1	1	92
Butter	1 T.	100	trace	trace	12
Cabbage, cooked	1 cup	30	2	6	trace
Cabbage, raw, finely shredded	1 cup	15	1	4	trace

	PORTION	CALORIES	PROTEIN	CARBOHY.	FAT
Cantaloupe	½ medium	60	1	14	trace
Carrots, cooked, cut	1 cup	45	1	10	trace
Carrots, raw	1 medium	20	1	5	trace
Catsup, tomato	1 T.	15	trace	4	trace
Cauliflower, cooked	1 cup	25	3	5	trace
Celery, raw, large stalk	One	5	trace	2	trace
Cheese, American or cheddar	1" cube	70	4	trace	6
Cheese, American, processed	1" cube	65	4	trace	5
Cheese, cottage, creamed	1 cup	260	33	7	10
Cheese, cottage, uncreamed	1 cup	170	34	5	1
Cheese, cream	1 T.	55	1	trace	5
Cheese, Parmesan, grated	2 T.	50	4	trace	4
Cheese, Swiss	1" cube	55	4	trace	4
Cherries, fresh, sweet	½ cup	40	1	13	trace
Chicken, fried	½ breast	155	25	1	5
Chicken, fried	1 leg	90	12	trace	4
Chicken, roasted	3 ounces	160	23	0	7
Chili con Carne, with beans	1 cup	335	19	30	15
Chili con Carne, without beans	1 cup	510	26	15	38
Cola type beverages	12 ounces	145	0	37	0
Coconut, dried, shredded, packed	1 cup	450	5	12	46
Consomme	1 cup	10	2	0	trace
Cookies, chocolate chip	One	50	1	6	3
Cookies, oatmeal	1 large	90	1	14	3
Corn, canned	1 cup	140	5	33	1
Corn flakes, plain	1 cup	100	2	21	trace
Corn muffins	1 medium	125	3	19	4
Cornmeal, dry	½ cup	440	11	91	4

	PORTION	CALORIES	PROTEIN	CARBOHY.	FAT
Cornstarch	1 T.	30			
Crackers, Ritz	One	15	trace	4	trace
Crackers, soda	One	25	trace	6	trace
Cranberries, fresh	1 cup	55	trace	14	trace
Cream, light	1 T.	30	1	1	3
Cream, sour	½ cup	245	4	5	24
Cream, heavy whipping	1 T.	50	trace	1	6
Cucumbers	1 medium	30	1	7	trace
Dates, dried, pitted	One	20	trace	6	trace
Eggplant, sliced	1 cup	50	2	12	trace
Eggs, scrambled	1 large	110	7	1	8
Eggs, hard-cooked	1 large	75	6	trace	6
Eggs, white only	1 large	15	4	trace	trace
Eggs, yolk only	1 large	60	3	trace	5
Figs, dried	1 large	60	1	15	trace
Fish sticks, breaded	5 sticks	200	19	8	10
Flour, wheat, all-purpose	1 cup	420	12	88	1
Frankfurters, cooked	One	170	7	1	15
Garbanzo beans (chick-peas), dry	1 cup	700	42	110	9
Grape Nuts	½ cup	200	5	46	trace
Grapefruit, white	½ medium	45	1	12	trace
Grapefruit juice, unsweetened	8 ounces	100	1	24	trace
Grapes (Muscat, Thompson, Tokay)	1 cup	95	1	25	trace
Haddock, fried	3 ounces	140	17	5	5
Ham, baked	3 ounces	245	18	0	19
Honey	1 T.	65	trace	17	0
Honeydew melon	½ medium	65	1	17	0

	PORTION	CALORIES	PROTEIN	CARBOHY.	FAT
Ice cream, chocolate	1 cup	300	5	33	16
Ice cream, vanilla	1 cup	290	6	28	14
Ice cream, sherbert	1 cup	260	2	59	2
Ice milk	1 cup	220	6	29	7
Lamb chop, with fat	4 ounces	400	25	0	33
Lamb chop, lean only	2.6 ounces	140	21	0	6
Lamb roast, leg	3 ounces	235	22	0	16
Leeks, cooked	3 medium	30	3	6	trace
Lemons, fresh	1 medium	20	1	6	trace
Lemon meringue pie, 9-inch	1/7	305	4	45	12
Lentils, dry	½ cup	340	25	60	1
Lettuce, compact	1 head	60	4	13	trace
Liver, beef, fried	2 ounces	130	15	3	6
Lobster, African	1 tail	300	20	1	24
Macaroni, enriched, cooked	1 cup	155	5	32	1
Margarine	½ cup	815	1	1	92
Margarine, whipped	½ cup	545	1	trace	61
Mayonnaise	1 T.	100	trace	trace	11
Melba toast	1 slice	25			
Milk, whole	8 ounces	160	9	12	9
Milk, skim, non-fat	8 ounces	90	9	12	trace
Milk, buttermilk	1 cup	90	9	12	trace
Milk, condensed, undiluted	1 cup	980	25	166	27
Milk, evaporated, undiluted	1 cup	345	18	24	20
Milk, powdered, nonfat, dried	1 cup	245	24	35	trace
Muffin, bran	1 medium	105			

	PORTION	CALORIES	PROTEIN	CARBOHY.	FAT
Muffin, English	1 medium	125			
Mushroon soup, cream of	1 cup	135	2	10	10
Mushrooms, canned	1 cup	40	5	6	trace
Mushrooms, sauteed, small	4-5	50	1	2	5
Mustard, prepared	1 T.	10			
Noodles, egg, cooked, enriched	1 cup	200	7	37	2
Oatmeal, cooked	1 cup	130	5	23	2
Olive Oil	1 T.	125	0	0	14
Olives, green	4 medium	15	trace	trace	2
Onions, raw, 2½-inch diameter	One	40	2	10	trace
Orange juice, fresh	8 ounces	110	2	26	1
Oranges, fresh	1 medium	65	1	16	trace
Pancakes, 4-inch diameter	One	60	2	9	2
Peaches, fresh	1 medium	35	1	10	trace
Peaches, canned in syrup	1 half	45	trace	12	trace
Peanut butter	1 T.	95	4	3	8
Peanuts, roasted, halves	½ cup	420	19	14	36
Pears, fresh	1 medium	100	1	25	1
Pears, canned in syrup	1 half	45	trace	12	trace
Peas, green, cooked	1 cup	115	9	19	1
Peppers, green, raw	1 medium	15	1	4	trace
Pickles, dill	1 large	10	1	1	trace
Pine nuts	12 to 14	100			
Pineapple, fresh	1 cup	75	1	19	trace
Plums, fresh	1 medium	25	trace	7	trace
Popcorn, popped with oil	1 cup	40	1	5	2

	PORTION	CALORIES	PROTEIN	CARBOHY.	FAT
Pork chops	3 ounces	260	16	0	21
Potato chips, 2" diameter	8 to 10	115	1	10	8
Potatoes, white, baked	1 medium	90	3	21	trace
Potatoes, French fried, 2x½x½"	Ten	155	2	20	7
Potatoes, sweet, baked	1 medium	155	2	36	1
Pretzels, thin twisted	One	25	1	5	trace
Prunes, cooked, unsweetened	5 medium	100	1	26	trace
Pumpkin, canned	1 cup	75	2	18	1
Raddishes, red, raw	4 medium	7	trace	2	trace
Raisins, seedless	½ cup	240	2	64	trace
Raspberries, red, fresh	1 cup	70	1	17	1
Rhubarb, cooked, sweetened	1 cup	385	1	98	trace
Rice, white, enriched, cooked	1 cup	225	4	50	trace
Ry-Krisp, double square	One	20	1	5	trace
Salad dressings, French or Russian	1 T.	60	trace	2	6
Salmon, pink, canned	3 ounces	120	17	0	5
Sauerkraut, canned	1 cup	45	2	9	trace
Sesame seeds, hulled	1 ounce	160	5	4	15
Shredded wheat	1 biscuit	90	2	20	1
Shrimp, canned	3 ounces	100	21	1	1
Soybeans, dry, whole	½ cup	315	38	25	17
Spaghetti, enriched, cooked	1 cup	155	5	32	1
Spinach, cooked	1 cup	40	5	6	1
Split pea soup	1 cup	145	9	21	3
Squash, summer, cooked, sliced	1 cup	30	2	7	trace
Squash, winter, baked, mashed	1 cup	130	4	32	1

	PORTION	CALORIES	PROTEIN	CARBOHY.	FAT
Strawberries, fresh	1 cup	55	1	13	1
Strawberries, frozen, sliced	1 cup	275	1	70	trace
Sugar, brown	1 cup	820	0	212	0
Sugar, powdered (confectioner's)	1 cup	460	0	119	0
Sugar, granulated	1 cup	770	0	199	0
Sugar, granulated	1 T.	40	0	11	0
Tangerines	1 medium	40	1	10	trace
Thousand Island dressing	1 T.	80	trace	3	8
Tomato juice, canned	8 ounces	45	2	10	trace
Tomato soup, cream of	1 cup	90	2	16	3
Tomatoes, raw, 3" diameter	One	40	2	9	trace
Tomatoes, canned	1 cup	50	2	10	1
Tuna, canned in oil, drained	3 ounces	170	24	0	7
Turkey, roasted	3 ounces	160	25	0	6
Veal cutlet, medium fat	3 ounces	185	23	0	9
Vegetable oil	1 T.	125	0	0	14
Walnuts, English	½ cup	400	13	10	38
Water chestnuts	Five	20			trace
Watermelon, 1½" thick slice	One	115	2	27	1
Wheat, flakes	1 cup	105	3	24	trace
Wheat germ, toasted	1 ounce	105	8	13	3
Wine, dessert	3 ounces	125	trace	32	0
Wine, table	3 ounces	75	trace	19	0
Yeast, dry, active	1 pkg.	20	3	3	trace
Yogurt, from skim milk	1 cup	125	8	13	4

A handy reference guide for those wishing to kick the cholesterol habit. It is important to stress that dietary cholesterol is obtained only from foods of animal origin. Foods of plant origin have no cholesterol. The American Heart Association recommends eating balanced meals which are low in saturated fat and cholesterol as one step in lowering the risk of heart attack. Fat-cholesterol controlled diets should aim at an average daily intake of 300 milligrams (mg.) of cholesterol. The following cholesterol figures are primarily based on current U.S. Department of Agriculture information and are given in milligrams of cholesterol. These figures are approximate and rounded-off.

	PORTION	CHOL.		PORTION	CHOL.
Bacon, crisp	2 slices	15	Cheese, cottage, creamed	1 cup	50
Beef, average all cuts	3 ounces	80	Cheese, cottage, uncreamed	1 cup	15
Beef, lean	3 ounces	75	Cheese, cream	1 T.	15
Beef, heart	3 ounces	230	Cheese, Edam	1 ounce	30
Bologna, all beef	1 slice	10	Cheese, Feta	1 ounce	15
Butter	1/2 cup	280	Cheese, Mozzarella	1 ounce	20
Butter	1 T.	35	Cheese, Muenster	1 ounce	25
Cake, devil's food, 9-inch diam.	1/16	30	Cheese, Parmesan, grated	1 T.	5
Cake, sponge, 10-inch diam.	1/12	160	Cheese, Provolone	1 ounce	30
Cake, yellow, 9-inch diam.	1/16	35	Cheese, Ricotta	1 ounce	15
Cereals, all		0	Cheese, Ricotta, part skim	1 ounce	10
Cheese, American, processed	1 ounce	25	Cheese, Swiss	1 ounce	30
Cheese, Blue or Roquefort	1 ounce	25	Cheese, Swiss, processed	1 ounce	25
Cheese, Camembert	1 ounce	35	Cheese spread, American	1 ounce	20
Cheese, Cheddar	1 ounce	30	Cheese substitute, "Cheez-ola"	1 ounce	1

	PORTION	CHOL.
Chicken, fried	1/2 breast	75
Chicken, fried	1 leg	45
Chicken a la king	1 cup	185
Chicken potpie, commercial	8 ounces	30
Clams, large	four	25
Cookies, brownie, homemade	one	15
Cookies, ladyfinger	four	155
Cornbread, from mix	1 muffin	30
Crab, canned	1 cup	160
Crab, fresh	1 cup	125
Cream, half and half	1 cup	105
Cream, light	1 T.	10
Cream, light	1 cup	160
Cream, heavy whipping	1 T.	20
Cream, non-dairy	1 T.	0
Cream, non-dairy, whipped	1 T.	0
Cream, sour	1/2 cup	75
Cream puffs with custard	one	190
Custard, baked	1 cup	280
Doughnuts, medium	one	15
Egg substitute, "Egg beaters"	1/4 cup	0
Eggs	1 large	250
Eggs, white only	1 large	0
Eggs, yolk only	1 large	250
Flour, all types		0
Frankfurters, all meat	one	35
Fruit, all		0

	PORTION	CHOL.
Haddock, cooked	3 ounces	50
Halibut, cooked	3 ounces	50
Ham, lean	3 ounces	75
Ice Cream, chocolate	1 cup	70
Ice Cream, regular 10% fat	1 cup	55
Ice Cream, rich, 16% fat	1 cup	85
Ice Cream, frozen custard	1 cup	95
Ice Cream, sherbet	1 cup	10
Ice Milk, hardened	1 cup	25
Ice Milk, soft-serve	1 cup	35
Lamb, average all cuts	3 ounces	85
Lamb, lean	3 ounces	75
Lard	1 T.	15
Lard	1 cup	195
Liver, beef	3 ounces	370
Liver, chicken	1 ounce	210
Lobster, meat only	3 ounces	70
Macaroni & Cheese, homemade	1 cup	40
Margarine, from veg. oil	1 T.	0
Margarine, diet	1 T.	0
Mayonnaise	1 T.	10
Mayonnaise	1 cup	155
Milk, whole	8 ounces	35
Milk, skim, non-fat	8 ounces	5
Milk, buttermilk	1 cup	5
Milk, condensed, undiluted	1 cup	105
Milk, evaporated, undiluted	1 cup	80

	PORTION	CHOL.
Muffins, English	one	0
Muffins, plain, 3-inch	one	20
Noodles, egg, cooked	1 cup	50
Noodles, chow mein	1 cup	5
Nuts, all		0
Pancakes, with egg & milk	6-inch	55
Peanut butter	2 T.	0
Pies, custard, 9-inch	1/8	120
Pies, lemon meringe, 9-inch	1/8	100
Pies, pumpkin, 9 inch	1/8	70
Pork, average all cuts	3 ounces	75
Pork, trimmed of fat	3 ounces	75
Potato salad, homemade	1 cup	35
Potatoes au gratin	1 cup	15
Potatoes, scalloped	1 cup	160
Puddings, chocolate, from mix	1 cup	30
Puddings, vanilla, homemade	1 cup	35
Rice pudding, with raisins	1 cup	30
Rice, Spanish, from mix	1 cup	25
Salad dressing, French	1 T.	0
Salmon, cooked	3 ounces	40
Salmon, pink, canned	3 ounces	30
Scallops	3 ounces	45
Shrimp, canned	3 ounces	125
Shrimp, large	six	50
Spaghetti & meat balls	1 cup	75
Sugars, all	1 T.	0

	PORTION	CHOL.
Summer sausage	1 slice	15
Tartar sauce	1 T.	7
Tuna, canned in oil	3 ounces	55
Tuna, canned in water	3 ounces	55
Turkey, light meat, skinned	3 ounces	65
Turkey, dark meat, skinned	3 ounces	85
Turkey, potpie, commerical	8 ounces	20
Veal, lean	3 ounces	85
Vegetable oils, all	1 T.	0
Vegetable shortening	1 T.	0
Vegetables, all		0
Waffles, with milk & egg	9-inch	120
Welsh rarebit	1 cup	70
White sauce, thin	1 cup	36
White sauce, medium	1 cup	33
White sauce, thick	1 cup	30
Whiskey	1 1/2 ounces	0
Wine	3 ounces	0
Yoghurt, non-fat	8 ounces	15
Yoghurt, plain	8 ounces	15

KITCHEN WEIGHTS & MEASURES

Fluid Measures

1 T.	= 3 teaspoons	= 1/2 ounce
1/8 cup	= 2 tablespoons	= 1 ounce
1/4 cup	= 4 tablespoons	= 2 ounces
1/3 cup	= 5 tablespoons plus 1 teaspoon	
1/2 cup	= 8 tablespoons	= 4 ounces
2/3 cup	= 10 tablespoons plus 2 teaspoons	
3/4 cup	= 12 tablespoons	= 6 ounces
1 cup	= 16 tablespoons	= 8 ounces
2 cups	= 1 pint	= 16 ounces
4 cups	= 2 pints = 1 qt.	= 32 ounces

Dry Measures

1 ounce = approx. 30 grams
1 pound = 16 ounces = 454 grams

For the cook's convenience, the recipes are listed by the name of recipe,
name of meat cut, and category of recipe (appetizer, soup, etc.).

C

N

O

P

T

W

Z

"Teach unto the people how they ought to live wisely
and honestly of their goods, and not to waste too
much before hand, lest they should want after."

From THE BOOK OF THRIFT
by James Bellot, 1589

"Nor love, nor honour, wealth, nor power
Can give the heart a cheerful hour
When health is lost"

John Gay, 1685-1731
FABLES

"Good nutrition is health's greatest ally."
Dr. Jim

We hope the recipes have pleased you enough that you will want to recommend this cookbook to others. If additional copies of this, or the companion budget-minded, health conscious book **THE MEATLESS MEAL GUIDE** (240 pages, illustrated and indexed), are unavailable at your book store, send check or money order in the amount of $4.50 per book to The Ryan Company. Postage and handling included. Please add sales tax if delivered in California.

THE RYAN COMPANY

2188 Latimer Lane   Los Angeles, Ca. 90024

Also available are two colorful blank books, **GOURMET MY WAY** and **THE GREAT COOK WRITES A BOOK**, for compiling your own cookbook. Your completed book may be sent to The Ryan Company for evaluation for publication. Send $2.35 for each book, check or money order.